CW01086270

Essays on lone trips, mountain-craft and other hill topics

Adam Watson

Publication of this book was aided by the generous sponsorship of Bert McIntosh of Crathes near Banchory in Scotland and McIntosh Plant Hire (Aberdeen) Ltd, Birchmoss, Echt, Westhill, Aberdeenshire AB32 6XL, www.mphltd.co.uk

Published by Paragon Publishing, 4 North Street, Rothersthorpe, Northants, NN7 3JB, UK

First published 2016
© Adam Watson 2016

All rights reserved. No part of this publication may be reproduced, stored in a retrieval system or transmitted in any form or by any means, electronic, mechanical, photocopying, recording or otherwise, without the prior written permission of the copyright owners.

Clachnaben, Crathes, Banchory, Aberdeenshire AB31 5JE, Scotland, UK adamwatson@uwclub.net

ISBN 978-1-78222-460-0

Book design, layout and production management by Into Print

www.intoprint.net +44 (0) 1604 832149

Printed and bound in UK, USA and Australia by Lightning Source

Front and back covers. Two lone trips in Baffin Island, Arctic Canada, 1953

Contents

Chapter 1. Dangerous thoughts on the mountain organisation-man (Etchachan Club Journal (Penthowff), 1975, 1–19)

The bureaucratic organisation-man, steadily increasing in numbers and authority, is already a common threat to the freedom of the individual. Whatever you do, be you farmer, student, factory worker, housewife with school children, you will have come across him, and probably many of your decisions and actions may be governed or at least influenced by him. I use the words 'organisation-man' because his main concern is to devise plans and structures for organising people. Of courses we do need some organisation men to improve and work for individual freedom and interests, but they are generally a very different kind of being from the bureaucratic organisation-man. Examples of them in the mountain world are those who recently re-organised the Etchachan Club or those who organised the Cairngorm Firemen (i.e. nickname for the Cairngorms Group, an informal conservation body that was a forerunner for the North East Mountain Trust). The difference is that they are usually doing these things in their spare time, because they believe in an ideal, an ideal whose furtherance will bring them no financial or other material gains and indeed will generally lose them money. By contrast, most bureaucratic organisation-men work in full-time or at least part-time jobs, whose active furtherance is likely to bring them promotion and other financial or material rewards. The projects that they accomplish usually entail far more thoroughness and work than spare-timers can muster, because the bureaucrat is doing it full or part-time, with many more resources behind him. Another important difference is that often the bureaucrat does not hold the subject of his current piece of work as an ideal. Indeed he may be interested in that subject only in so far as his current work now happens to impinge on it; it may not have done so a month or a year ago, or ahead when some new project will have landed on his desk.

One major defect which results from all this is that the bureaucratic organisation-man often comes to regard his plan, structure or organisation as more important than the aim which it is intended to serve. It frequently grows to be such a substitute for the real thing that the means become more important to him than the ends.

Students of these problems will recognise this as a common symptom of 'Peter's Principle' where so often the bureaucrat is promoted a step beyond his level of competence. In industry, local government, and other big organisations his usual catchword is efficiency, but in the mountains his thinking takes on a variety of other nebulous forms where the efficiency is seldom defined or tested, the aims are often poorly stated and the starting assumptions are usually not stated or tested in any way.

I will now describe, one by one, a few of the various forms in which the bureaucratic mountain organisation-man has appeared increasingly in recent years. The thoughts which I state about them are merely personal opinions, as untested as some of the beliefs that I will be questioning. Nevertheless the central point I hold is that new beliefs, changes and regulations which reduce the individual freedom of many of us should be tested and proved before being widely accepted and put into regular use. It is therefore entirely justifiable for critics to argue against the lack of any testing of these new beliefs and innovations, even if they can provide only personal opinions and no hard evidence or proof against them. The onus lies squarely on the innovators to justify their claims by evidence, not on those who question them and who ask for this evidence, which is all too frequently lacking.

The developer organisation-man

Since 1960 and increasingly in the 1970s, he has become the greatest threat to wild hills and coast, and thus to the Scottish climber's individual freedom and appreciation of these places. If he is not curbed, little of the most outstanding country in Scotland will be left for future generations to enjoy, and they will condemn the selfishness of the 1970s and our failure to stop it.

Along with the actual developers who make the profits out of their development, and the landowners who make profits from selling them the land, we can classify the local councillors who are keen on development. There are also the tourist and development officers and boards, and the university men who get grants from these official organisations and who write glossy, eye-catching surveys which help airy-fairy ideas to become powerful bandwagons and later to become official county plans and real developments. In our part of Scotland the report *Cairngorm Area*, with its proposals for a Feshie road, a Tilt road, a Derry outdoor centre, ski-lifts here and there and many other developments scattered over most parts of the Cairngorms, contains more than enough to let us see the dangers. Other major proposals in the last few years are a road through Lairig Ghru, and in other parts of Scotland a summer and winter tourist resort on Aonach Mor and a big skiing ground on Ben Wyvis. We have room to mention only a few examples; a complete list would fill the journal.

These developments and others like them would spoil the wilderness value of large areas of our Scottish hill country and detract from the feelings of wildness and remoteness that most climbers cherish. But they are also likely to bring other less obvious curbs on the climber's individual freedom. What has happened on the Cairn Gorm plateau is a pointer to this in future. Once you have large numbers of tourists wandering around on high ground because access has become very easy due to new roads and chair lifts, more people are liable to get lost and run into other difficulties. The reports of the Countryside Commission for Scotland, worrying about the inadequate experience, poor equipment and very young ages of many of these tourists, have called for a wardening service on the plateau, to guide and look after visitors. Many more people bring new problems that require more regulations and thus less freedom.

The laird organisation-man

He can be a full-time variety but in practice most are only part-time organisation-men. He has long been characterised by a strong tendency to work as a single individual at the top of his own hierarchy, but as his problems mount he is increasingly beginning to band together with others for strength. Never keen on the public coming on to his land, in more feudal decades he often just said 'No' and even tried it in the courts over long established rights of way.

A few are a still obstructive, as a glance at the annual report of the Scottish Rights of Way Society will show. But this old attitude is no longer popular or wise in 1975, especially with so much talk nowadays about public ownership, what will Labour do, what will the SNP do? One of the modern, more acceptable ways for a laird to say 'No' is to invoke conservation. His argument goes that land is being overused by too many climbers and ramblers, so we must have rules, and even bye-laws forbidding access. Hence the so-called 'access agreements' are created, which in reality deny us nearly all the freedom that we have long possessed. As a conservationist myself, I can see the need to have rules, and in some cases possibly even to forbid access to certain outstanding areas, but they are few in number and small in extent, and they need not involve restrictions at most times of year. By contrast, some lairds wish access to be restricted and in a few cases even banned for most or all of the year. The fact is that this is seldom for wildlife but for grouse shooting and deer shooting. All right, these are economic uses for land that is often too infertile for anything else. But let us first have some evidence that these land-uses really are being damaged by climbers and walkers. Here, the little research that has so far been done shows evidence against the restriction point of view.

Meanwhile some lairds who would like to restrict access on supposed conservation grounds have been taking other actions that are unquestionably damaging to conservation interests. A good example is their bulldozing of cheap, poorly-made hill tracks for their own grouse shooting and deer stalking, tracks which scar fine landscapes, damage rare communities of alpine tundra vegetation, cause erosion, and paradoxically make access to tourists even easier than it was! Others have sold some of their land at great profit to make way for hotels, private housing schemes and other such developments which greatly add to the pressure of visitors upon the countryside.

A new risk is that some lairds, fearful of the attitudes of SNP and Labour, and worrying about what the public now think of private individuals owning vast tracts of countryside, may jump too hastily and without enough care into new developments that they start so to improve their public relations. For instance, an increasingly common idea is to open up small parts of their estates to far more visitors than ever before, by providing new car parks, toilets, picnic places and information centres, and by giving all this plenty of publicity in radio, press, tourist leaflets, and local hotels. Although this may be useful at carefully chosen places down in the main valley, such developments are inappropriate if sited at road ends in the tops of the glens. There they can add unnecessarily to visitor pressure in more fragile environments where people cause more damage. As a result, these problems are in turn more likely to lead to extra regulations on camping and other matters, curbing the freedom that climbers already have there.

The worthwhile causes and do-gooder organisation-man

This is a spare-time, part-time, or occasionally full-time variety of the mountain-organisation-man, very keen on erecting monuments which are all too likely to out-survive him. These are the men who organise the building of hill indicators which spoil your interest in working out the view for yourself, who organise the erection of plaques on the four highest peaks of the Cairngorms to commemorate the centenary of Rotherham County Council, or memorial tablets scattered here and there over the North-east Highlands noting the death of Tom, Dick, or Harry. They also put up lines of cairns, which are supposed to guide the incompetent, but which sometimes get the incompetent thoroughly lost and lead them on to the wrong side of the hill many extra miles away. Another example is the Curran Bothy, which was erected partly to give a services group something to do and partly to commemorate a member of that group. The Camasunary road and bridge was another of several such cases involving the services. However well intentioned these schemes may have been, the fact remains that they were planned and carried out without enough consultation with climbers, mountain rescuers and conservation interests, and in the case of the erection of the Curran, without receiving the planning permission that is required by law. It is therefore not surprising that most of them have led to controversy and trouble for the promoters. Furthermore, these schemes reduce individual freedom and spoil the wilderness quality of our hills.

An example of an organisation that was set up for worthwhile jobs in the hills is the 'Bailies of Bennachie'. Some of their original aims, removing litter and repairing paths, are admirable. But there are signs of a change, probably due to the Bailies confining themselves to too small an area, and partly to their building

up a big organisation and much publicity with the press and local VIPs, out of all proportion to conservation needs on Bennachie. They have already erected a summit indicator on the Mither Tap and have considered another on Oxen Craig. There is talk of new paths and other facilities, which will attract extra visitors who would not go but for the new facilities and publicity. There is a risk that 'worthwhile causes' organisations build up so much that they cannot get enough to do on their original aims and instead have to devise new schemes to keep their members busy. The new schemes may well prove harmful, and may in the end put at risk what the organisation set out to conserve.

Cairngorm Fireman organisation-man

A spare-time variety, this is a recent howling infant on the mountain scene. Perhaps it may bawl louder in future as its muscles grow stronger. The conservationist has appeared mainly as a reaction to damage and threats to conservation interests by the developer organisation-man. The conservationist could be a threat to the climber's individual freedom, even though on most issues he and the climber agree. The only conflict at present has come over the need to restrict access at certain times of year to certain places, for example some cliffs where uncommon birds of prey are nesting. There is conflict over this at two or three cliffs in Speyside but the problem does not arise in Deeside and the Angus glens where the cliffs that birds of prey frequent are all broken vegetated crags or else steep but very short walls, none of which is much used by climbers. Conflict between climbers and conservationists has also occurred over sea-cliffs in Wales and elsewhere, where populations of sea-birds which are already decreasing or are seriously at risk from pollution must now suffer an extra hazard from disturbance by climbers during the nesting season. The conflict has been lessened by the climbers agreeing to avoid those parts of the cliffs which support many sea-birds, during the breeding season of the colonies. Again, here in the north-east I can foresee no problem, as all the big sea-bird colonies are on cliffs that the climbers do not use. This might change in future if the pressure for exploration leads to so-far unclimbed cliffs, but there is no sign of this at present, either because these cliffs are vegetated or dirty with droppings, or else are extremely steep walls of unreliable rock, again well whitewashed with droppings.

A possible conflict in future might come if conservationists wish to develop certain habitats that should be in the Cairngorms, but are not there because of deliberate burning and long over-grazing by too many deer and sheep. An example of this might be to develop forest down on the valley bottoms or along the glen sides; this would not be just a pine forest but a diverse kind of northern forest more like the boreal forests of Eurasia and North America. Another example might be to encourage the growth of a diverse boreal scrub of birch and willow above the tree line, a kind of habitat which has virtually gone from Scotland. If' these habitats are to be developed, it might entail forbidding all camping, and perhaps even forbidding all access during the critical early stages of establishment, so as to prevent fire. But this would be unlikely to happen except on small sample parts of the Cairngorms which climbers seldom, if ever, visit anyway. If it can be explained to everybody that it is in the long-term public interest to re-create samples of the kind of habitats that Scotland is poverty-stricken in because of centuries of degrading misuse of our hill land, then I think the public is likely to agree to reasonable, fully explained restrictions. I think the climber will agree too, provided that his main interests are sympathetically considered and that access to his main climbing grounds is safeguarded. What he will not accept, and rightly, is the banning of all access over huge areas at most or at all times of year, with no good evidence for the ban, and here the conservationist agrees with him.

But this is enough on the unusual items where the conservationist and the Etchachan Club climber might possibly conflict in future. On most of the issues described in this article they agree, so it is not surprising that Cairngorm Firemen and Etchachan Club members are often the very same individuals! The new Etchachan Club is very different and a much better variety than the old one. The renewal began in early 1974, exactly when the Firemen also came to together to form their new group. Cooperation between the two is excellent. Here is an example. The tipping of rubbish near one of the best climbing grounds at South Cove was stopped recently. It would not have been, but for this cooperation and the similarity of outlook by some people in both organisations.

The outward-bounder organisation-man

This is the outdoor-education man or adventure-training man, usually a full-time variety. He is increasing in numbers faster than any other type apart from the mountain rescuer who has to cope with many of the resulting tragedies. Outdoor education is rapidly becoming a fairly big business. Every county must have its own staff and facilities, reaching strange new heights in 1974 with Argyll, whose county council were considering the urgent need for an outdoor centre in this, one of the most rural, wild and thinly populated parts of Scotland. Another example was in the Aberdeen *Press & Journal* on 17 January, where a photograph at Ellon Academy showed a group of children and adults attending a course on the theory of hill craft, introduced by Aberdeen County Community Service. Similar courses were also to be held at Aboyne and Huntly, yet these are in fact ideal places for a child to explore the countryside for himself. Other examples of these new schemes, backed by expensive payments from the rates, appear frequently in the newspapers. Chief of the untested beliefs that are widely accepted is that outdoor education on the hills is good for building the character of children.

Organised education in such an individual sport as climbing is sure to fetter us with rules and reduce freedom and wonder. I will use a personal example as a contrast. When I was eight years old at Turriff, Bennachie was my ultimate, a mysterious hill in the sky beyond the rolling farmland of Badenscoth. I explored alone to the tiny hills of Deveronside, like Mountblairy, from whose flat top I gazed in tremendous excitement at the view across the blue Moray Firth to the cone of Morven in far Caithness. These were the days of grand achievement. Later there came the lower Cairngorms in summer, then the higher ones, then the winter Cairngorms, then bigger mountains in Iceland and Norway, then vast unexplored space in arctic Canada. This progression of personal exploration and excitement had lasted fifteen years. Equipment for the first nine of them was tacketty boots and old jackets and coats. Many of us in the Etchachan Club had a similar introduction to the hills.

Compare this with what now happens in organised education where children may have to do compulsory climbing on artificial 'rock' walls as part of their physical training whether they like it or not, where those who wish the outdoor education that is offered are handed the latest full equipment free, are given lectures and detailed practical instruction on navigation and other aspects of climbing, are soon given hard rock-climbing or skiing, and are taken to the high hills of Scotland in winter within a year of their starting, all as part of their school curriculum. This must spoil any feeling of personal exploration for them, and greatly reduce the number of years when their excitement and imagination would be continually matching their expanding horizons. Moreover it is likely to make a child dissatisfied with anything other than the high hills. He would be unlikely to bother with the country at his back door, the country which he can reach quickly and in all weathers. Yet here in the north-east this back-door country offers a wealth of variety of coastal cliffs, beaches, estuaries, woods, rivers, lochs, moorlands, low hills, wildlife and human history and culture which is rich even on a world scale and which provides exploration beyond any lifetime.

What happened before and during the disaster at the Feith Buidhe on Cairn Gorm in 1971 was in many ways typical of wrong attitudes engendered by the outward-bounder organisation-man. Nor was this an unusual case. There are plenty of other good examples from the Cairngorms, and in the last two years from Snowdonia and elsewhere. The establishment's stock reaction to any trouble is 'They did the right thing, and stuck well to their earlier instruction', no matter how idiotic their behaviour was. Another reaction is to say more refuges are needed, better refuges with bells and lights, radios for each party and so on. The freedom of ordinary climbers is endangered by some of these reactions, like the proposal for a 'harbour-master of the hills' who could sanction or veto your wish to go on the hill, as called for by (Liberal?) Member of Parliament Russell Johnston after the disaster at the Feith Buidhe, and again in 1975 after several accidents in Inverness-shire.

After being an expert witness at the Public Inquiry on the Feith Buidhe disaster, I helped write an article which described the lessons that organised youth parties could learn from the disaster. Although it finished with several rules about what not to do, and thus with less freedom, this in no way conflicts with my general desire to fight against rules. In fact, I would like to see no organised parties of school children go to the high Cairngorms at all, summer or winter, as part of their formal, publicly paid school education, simply because it must spoil their individual exploration. The rules in that article were suggested as possibilities, entirely on the regrettable assumption that such courses and parties are here to stay. Also, I saw a clear distinction between the need for stringent safety and rules for leaders in charge of other people's children who were on the hill as part of their school education, and the need for as few rules and as much freedom as possible for individuals or groups of individuals, whether child or adult, going out of their own free will.

A recent report on safety in outdoor activities, issued by Aberdeen County Council, was enlightening in the way that it mentioned exposure in winter. The members of a party were urged to go in pairs, where each person would periodically examine the other member of his pair for early signs of exposure. Such a suggestion for children seems likely to encourage psychological feelings of exposure which might well lead to real physical exposure. Above all, such reports are likely to engender a wrong attitude to the experience of being on the hill. In a long account about equipment and exposure, almost nothing was said about the wonderful feelings or experiences of beautiful scenery, interesting weather and wildlife, humility, and oneness with nature that can come from a day on the hill. To be fair, I must admit that these aspects were not in the remit of the working party who wrote the report; the working party was asked to discuss safety. Nevertheless this, in the absence of as much or greater reporting on the other aspects, is bound to engender the wrong balance in the child's attitudes. I will go further and say that the child or adult who is deeply aware of these other aspects is thereby likely to be far safer on the hill than the child or adult who knows little about them even though he may have been given much formal instruction on safety from courses or from a report.

During the Public Inquiry on the Cairn Gorm Disaster, a leading person in outdoor education was asked why the fated excursion had not been vetoed. His answer was that excursions to the high hills in winter were not cancelled because there would be nothing for the parties to do lower down. Yet, lower down is the country of Strath Spey, so outstandingly rich in its variety of low hills, forests, lochs and wildlife, and with so much interesting evidence of our human history.

The statement about having nothing to do indicates the narrowness of outlook that too often occurs due to the outward-bounder organisation-man.

The mountain rescuer organisation-man

Here is a rapidly increasing variety organised in tightly disciplined groups which show considerable rivalry and territorial behaviour towards one another's intrusions on one another's home ground. In most cases he is only a part-time bureaucrat. Increasingly nowadays he makes condemnations when any party or person offends his rules. The condemnations and rules are delivered with conviction and with the authority that comes from exaggerated respect by press and TV. Unfortunately, press and TV too often like sensationalism, which is readily available to them in mountain rescues. Examples of the condemnations are to criticise anybody who walks, skis or climbs alone, especially in winter, or who goes up the hill with no compass or map. Examples of the rules are to make sure you carry full survival gear in winter, and summer/ winter, to fill up a route form saying where you are going and when and where you'll be back. There are many other rules. Much of this is probably valuable for those with neither experience nor humility who go straight to Glen Coe or the high Cairngorms in winter without having tried the lower hills in summer. But we have now reached a stage where it may be unwise to go on increasing the blanket rules and condemnations without carefully considering where all this could eventually lead.

Quite a number of climbers in the Etchachan Club and other clubs have from time to time ignored some of these rules in the past, and still do. Occasionally they like going alone, day or night, summer or winter, on skis or on foot. In summer they sometimes do not carry a map on the Cairngorms, or a compass unless they are perhaps interested in getting back-bearings for locating distant peaks in the view. Some of them may seldom carry a map and compass even in winter, except when walking or skiing over snow-covered plateaux where white-outs and cornices are a risk. A few believe that the best practice in navigation comes from navigating as much as possible without a map or compass. This does not mean that they advocate that going to the hills without a map or compass is a good thing for people in general, and in fact they themselves would not do so on hills that they did not know well. It merely means that there are a few climbers who know a particular area of hill country so extremely well that map and compass become generally redundant. They do not carry full survival gear. They have never filled up a route card and do not intend to start doing so.

They think that those who have most feeling for the hills and who sense humility and wonder there, are those who are unfettered by rules. Though they may sometimes ignore the bureaucratic organisation-man's rules, these are his words, not theirs. In their terms, ignoring these rules means freedom to enjoy and become part of their hill environment, in the same way as their forebears did before these rules were invented or the organisation-man first appeared. They do not ignore the rules deliberately to be "anti" this or that. Instead, their view of the freedom of enjoying the hills has been and is natural and positive; to them, it is the organisation-man's outlook which is negative. Though greatly surpassed by the numbers and resources of the organisation-man and his supporters, they are an increasing company, for example many past and present Etchachan Club members. However, on the subjects of rules and mountain-rescue organisation-men, they are a set of rather unorganised individualists and they tend to lack influence, all because they tend to be suspicious of the idea that an organisation-man, however well intentioned, should push their case or organise them! But one of these days they may have to push their case, or their freedom night be swamped. The mountain-rescuer organisation-man has had so much publicity that many in the general public often now look unkindly on climbers, and back any ideas for curbing climbers' freedom and for the police regulating whether or not a given party should be allowed to go where they want on a given occasion.

If the rescuer organisation-man does not give serious thought to the recent trend towards many more rules and criticisms, then an increasing back-lash is likely. You fill find an early example of it in Robin Campbell's words in the SMC Journal editorial (Vol 30, pp. 1-3), which should be read in full by everybody interested in this problem. That editorial is not the only such piece that he has written. In the SMC Journal (Vol 30, p. 90), he again made a pertinent comment when introducing the annual list of Scottish mountain accidents, pointing out that many of these are not real accidents at all but merely incidents. He wrote, 'Many of the incidents are unremarkable and would have gone unnoticed in former, less complicated times when benightment, for example, was looked on as part and parcel of normal climbing and leaving of detailed route-plans unthinkable.'

An example of this appears in the SMC Journal (Volume 30, p. 286) in a report on Scottish Mountain Accidents 1973. The report reads: '31st July – Hamish Brown (39), Kinghorn, Fife, with party of four, left cars at roadside Inchnadamph and at Skiag on 30th July, walked to Loch Skiag and camped two nights. No indication of route or duration of stay left with anyone. Proprietor of hotel raised alarm with local member of Dundonnell M.R.T. Man hours of search – 40. Kinloss M.R.T. also called out, but party returned in good shape'. I cannot think of anybody less likely to get into difficulty at the end of July near Inchnadamph than Hamish Brown. The editorial in the SMC Journal (Volume 30, 1973, p193) about this incident gives appropriate comment: 'Personally, we feel there is a need for more circumspect action on the part of the rescue authorities. We believe that there is evidence in these reports to sustain such a point of view, but as the years go by the rescue authorities seem to become more trigger-happy, not less'.

Now the hotel keeper in the Inchnadamph incident was presumably also trigger-happy, but the blame cannot justifiably be placed on such people. One problem is that the whole mountain rescue scene has had so much publicity, especially in the last few years, that we now have a trigger-happy atmosphere in general, which affects members of the public as well as members of rescue teams. Because everything that they do comes under such a glare of publicity we must also sympathise with the dilemma that the rescue teams are in. If they stop being trigger-happy they are liable to find severe criticism for being too late and dilatory on occasions when a supposed harmless incident turns out in reality to be real trouble. Achieving the right balance is not easy, but recently the balance has verged more towards the trigger-happy side.

The influence of the mountain rescuer organisation-man extends far in some other ways. Estates freely allow his access during training sessions, through locked gates that are barred to climbers. Remote barns become private, locked, well fitted bothies to be used

by him and nobody else. Helicopters on rescue practice cause wholly unnecessary damage to fragile arctic-alpine vegetation in places of outstanding national value, and seriously disturb and frighten wild animals.. Tracked vehicles on practice rip up vegetation and hill paths, which in turn leads to soil erosion. Aerials, huts and roads for mountain rescue disfigure more hills. Lowering a mock casualty down a cliff became a part of Braemar Week, extending the laid-on entertainment for tourists, and adding further to the sensationalism and over-publicity that already exist with mountain rescues. Current television advertisements, to attract new recruits for the police, add far more to this over-publicity by showing spectacular pictures of policemen doing mountain rescue work, although in fact not one in a hundred of the new recruits in Scotland is likely to be heavily involved with mountain rescue.

The need for extra money for much more expensive rescue teams has led to sponsored walks by scores or even hundreds of people tramping across the Capel Mounth, the Lairig Ghru or over to the Shelter Stone, thus bringing heavy use and probably more erosion to fine old paths which are already suffering badly from over-use and lack of repairs. The mountain rescuers are on hand in case any of the walkers drops litter or gets sore feet. Most if not all of the walkers would never have gone there but for the current, curious popularity of taking part in a-sponsored walk, a human activity that seems more negative and purposeless than most. A mass sponsored walk will fail to give the participants a good appreciation of our hills and what they have to offer, and will instead engender a distorted and artificial feeling.

I could go on, and am tempted to explore the subject of rivalry and territorial behaviour of the mountain rescue teams, as it would certainly make an interesting study illustrating man's inherent tendencies to tribal group behaviour and to hierarchical dominance behaviour, but I had better stop or I will lose my mountain rescuer friends, who may leave me for the hoodie crows and the foxes if ever I break a leg while out alone on the hill: if so, no doubt I might begin to regret this article! But I would also regret the passing of those years before the organisation-man appeared, when the climber who did have an accident in the Cairngorms, Clova or Lochnagar was likely to be rescued by a scratch team of his friends, hot foot from Aberdeen.

Fundamentally the problem is one of numbers of people, and indeed the same comment is fundamental to all the other sections of this article. If only a few people go to the hills for their own enjoyment, of their own free will, there is less publicity if anything goes wrong, and there is -no need for elaborate mountain rescue. But if the services, the county councils, the tourist organisations, and numerous other official bodies encourage and arrange for many more people to go to the hills for reasons other than their own personal enjoyment (e.g. character-building, toughening-up, outdoor education etc.), then greater publicity, more public concern, elaborate rescue and many new rules become inevitable. The freedom of the free-will climber is an unfortunate casualty. But the blame for this lies not on the elaborate rescue teams which are now necessary, but on the diffuse official system that has produced and attracted to the hills the greater numbers of people who now need rescuing.

In discussing the mountain rescuer and the outward-bounder organisation-men, I am indirectly criticising some of my friends. However, I know that they are well aware of these criticisms by working them out in their own minds independently over the last year or two, during the very recent short period when these problems have began to be obvious. The fact that they like their jobs, which brought them to the hill country and to the climbing that means so much to them, is sometimes in conflict with occasional niggling and increasing criticisms in their own minds. We sympathise with the dilemmas that they are often in, and realise that it is a lot easier for free-will outsiders like us in the Etchachan Club to discuss these problems publicly. Also we realise that within their own official organisations they bring an influence for good, perhaps stronger than any that outsiders like us can bring. In any case, they are in a very different category from the powerful bureaucratic organisation-men, such as many of the developers, who are untroubled by any such dilemmas, who have no personal liking for the hill country and who regard it merely as a site for making money. Upon them the most criticism must go, which is why they are described first in this article.

Finale

I made the title of this article *Dangerous thoughts on the mountain organisation-man*. I did so because such thoughts are too seldom been put into words in public, but above all because many powerful bureaucratic organisation-men regard criticism of their big schemes as somehow immoral and selfish, since these schemes are devised with what they think are many good intentions and many high principled reasons. They have had a long innings their own way. Since 1973 we have come into a period with a great upsurge of objection to the bureaucratic organisation-man. Now we hear more often of decentralisation, individual rights and freedom, public inquiries, and 'No' to Common Market, Drumbuie, Concorde and Channel tunnel. Many action groups, individuals and publications now resist the bureaucratic organisation-man and his schemes. On the mountain scene, we are becoming aware of a similar upsurge of opposition. Fortunately, so many dissenters are now beginning to appear that the dangerous thoughts may soon be common-place ones.

Chapter 2. Seton Gordon compared with some recent writers on the Cairngorms

How do Seton Gordon's books such as *The Cairngorm Hills of Scotland* (1925) compare with more recent writers on the Cairngorms and Highland wildlife? Here I discuss this, selecting four of the main books. I exclude Desmond Nethersole-Thompson's specific bird monographs, other technical books, and guides. I omit books published since 1990, to avoid offence to living authors, and the likelihood of judgements being considered premature. Time will tell.

Some general books on Highland wildlife in the last few decades emphasised difficulties in observing and scarce observations. Emphasis on discomfort or difficulties, especially involving authors, signifies lack of deep expertise in observing wildlife. Some authors seem more interested in portraying themselves than in understanding hills and wildlife sympathetically. They show egotistical anthropocentric attitudes.

In my experience and that of other observers whom I respect, those who have studied wildlife from childhood and are vigilant almost never mention difficulties. They do not dwell on these when in one another's company on or off the hill. Instead, they often discuss field-craft, such as how a bird can mislead those trying to find its nest, or the need for showing respect for the nest and for other aspects of studying wildlife without affecting the wildlife adversely. The keenest will explain why they did not see something that another observer noticed first, or may ask the other observer how he noticed it first. Some have made remarkable published contributions. This includes several who had full-time jobs in other fields and could observe wildlife only in their spare time.

Several authors have written books on the Cairngorms and their wildlife since Seton Gordon's classic in 1925, but much of this has been too contrived. From my experience of certain authors, I know that their interest in the Cairngorms was fairly superficial. Too many overstated and dwelt on frequent bad weather, dangers, treacherous ice, dangerous rivers, and anthropocentric romantic discussions on the landscape's deeper meaning.

There is the associated approach in books, articles, radio and television where the interest is not in wildlife, but instead dwells upon people, hill-walking, climbing, skiing, hill-running, sponsored walks, challenge walks, etc. In this approach, danger and risk to life and limb are emphasised, along with the challenge of reducing the time taken, and associated phrases such as attacking, battling, and conquering a route or summit. A characteristic here is the stress on dangerous ice, treacherous weather, stealthy scree, and other such anthropocentric nonsense. This indicates writers who appear to wish to tell readers about themselves more than the wildlife or the hills. I hope an attitude of greater humility without anthropocentric attitudes may appeal more to those who think for themselves, and certainly it fits the Cairngorms and their wildlife. 'Wilderness walks' in television and publications are foreign to a deep appreciation of wilderness, which is an appreciation more akin to a solitary and quasi-religious experience.

W.A. Poucher

An early post-war book was W.A. Poucher's *A Camera in the Cairngorms* (1947). A mountaineer, Poucher had already written 10 books on British hills, based on photographs with some text. His Cairngorms book described a short trip in spring. I found the photographs muddy in tone and often not sharp. The text involved straightforward descriptions of hills and main routes, written by an experienced man who was unafraid of the hills and enjoyed them.

Richard Perry

Another notable book was Richard Perry's *In the High Grampians* (1948). It concentrated on wildlife, especially birds and mammals. He wrote some good descriptions of hill, glen, weather and wildlife, old farming townships and place names (though with some errors in Gaelic spelling), and local folk. His best descriptions are of plants, animals and weather on low ground, where he clearly felt at home. He lived near Drumguish east of Kingussie.

However, he overstated the difficulties of watching birds on high ground, and the (in his terms) continual mist and other bad weather daily for weeks in summer. This, he wrote, prevented his visits there. He saw remarkably few ptarmigan, dunlin, dotterel, and especially snow buntings, and certainly far fewer than the numbers that I knew to be there in these years. A colleague of mine who studied snow buntings said "Perry certainly missed a lot on the high tops". Perry added to the incorrect notion that hill birds were scarce and hard to find. Seeing dotterel displaying on Braeriach plateau but finding nests much lower, he wrote that they displayed in one place, like other species at a lek, but nested a long way further down. This was false inference, for he had overlooked nesting birds high up and had not seen them displaying low down. The notion of a lek in dotterel flocks was also incorrect.

Perry was awed and afraid of the high hills, especially in winter, but also in summer. Graphically he described a summer day when he became lost in fog on Braeriach, which signified his poor navigation. A few examples of his awe, and of anglicisations and other defects appear below.

p.9, the Vale of Rothiemurchus.

p.21, About snow on the hills. this cold, dead world.

p.34, For sixteen consecutive days from late May to early-June strong warm winds and heavy showers made fieldwork unprofitable outside the shelter of the woods.

p.94 a slag-heap 2,781 feet in height and a mile across the top.

p.112-113, Although 1943–44 was the second consecutive open winter in Badenoch, it was not until the end of March that the stalker's path had thawed out sufficiently to offer any possibility of my being able to gain the summit of Carn Ban Mor.

p.113, For some time I cast about for a way through, or round, the snowfield: but, with the clouds showing no sign of lifting, it was evident that nothing would be gained by any attempt to climb higher.

p.114, the additional strain of some thousands of feet of climbing and, worse, descending, and the severity of the weather conditions....I saw that every day's expedition would have to be planned to dovetail with fair weather, and with the necessary interval of rest between two such expeditions....Ten days elapsed before the weather proved favourable for a second attempt....Today, the path disappeared into a deep snowfield filling the apparently perpendicular allt of Ciste Mearad....It was slippery going up the last, almost sheer, 700 feet.

p.117, in the days and months to come, I opened up more and more of the Cairngorms, and met with new and unexpected forms of life, faunal and floral, on these uncongenial wastes....This was the last assault I was able to make on the tops for three weeks, for a period of westerly winds and rains set in.

p.118, I was able to make my first ascent as early as March 7, after four months' imprisonment in the lowlands.

p.119, I failed to locate it, and ended up in a maze of rocky cairns and pits that made the north and east edge of the moss almost impassable.

p.121, a fortnight elapsed before a calm and warmer day enabled me to put in one of my longest and most gruelling days on the tops....In the north-east corner of the moss I stumbled into that terrible country of outcrops and lochans.

p.123, (of An Garbh Choire on Braeriach) Soundless, life-less, sun-less   down the northern sidings to Loch Coire an Lochain in its naked pit at the shelving base of a 1,500-foot broken red scree.

p.124, just where the ascent became almost perpendicular up a grassy siding to the ultimate wall of crag the path did indeed peter out.

p.126, Summer is long in coming to the high tops and does not linger. A brief three months from late May to early August, and the remaining nine months of the year offer the naturalist barely enough material to justify such disproportionate expenditure of time and physical energy, when this is accounted against the time and energy that might have been expended more profitably and certainly more comfortably, if not as excitingly, in the glens and pine forests.

p.129, With May past, I did not see very much more of dotterel, or indeed of any mountain birds this first season, for the weather in June and July was atrocious.

p.133, For twelve days I fretted in the strath, before a fine morning dawned   this was the sum total of my notes for the day – and for thirteen subsequent days of perpetual cloud.

p.134, It was now a calendar month since I had seen any dotterel   of snow buntings I had seen nothing in either season.

p.135, June had been a most unlucky month. The continuous bad weather in 1944 and 1945 had permitted only five expeditions to the tops, and four of these had been ruined by rain and cloud.

p.141, This, I reflected, was only my twentieth expedition to the tops – not much to boast of for close on five hundred days' residence in the Grampians. But, then, I was living in Drumguish, not camping in the hills, and from the very first ascent it had been obvious that the only efficient way to work the tops was by camping on them for two or three months at a time, as Nethersole-Thompson had done. No naturalist could hope to make a worth-while study of any mountain species by seizing his opportunity on the rare fine days, and then wasting from four to eight hours, and much of his energy, in climbing to and from his objective. (I also mistakenly believed this in the late 1940s and early 1950s, but later realised that it is incorrect).

p.146, those awful corries above Glen Giusachan.

p.147, For a fortnight after that night out in the Horseman's Corrie I was strath-bound with bad weather.

p.148, the crumbling stack of the Devil's Point.

p.149, The gloomy defile of Glen Giusachan....The traveller through this almost subterranean pass through the Cairngorms from Glen Dee to Glen Feshie, as wild a pass as that of the Lairig Ghru, hurries to escape from these intolerably oppressive iron-bound walls of cliff and scree and the fearfully broken overhanging crags of the Devil's Point and Beinn Bhrotain....high above the impassable torrent-bed in the narrow and sinuous gorge below.

p.159, By the middle of September 1945 my old enemy Brae Riach was a brindled tawny, grey.

In early 1951 my father and I spent a weekend at Newtonmore and had a fine ski tour on the Monadh Liath. In my diary I wrote that in poor weather next day:- We went along to see author Richard Perry who now stays here. He said among other things that "there hadn't been a good day for skiing this winter". What nonsense! He is writing a book on red deer, about their life but "not a scientific life history, only the life history", he said, whatever that means. In fact it had been the best winter for ski touring that I had seen since 1944, and I have never seen one as good since.

Valdemar Axel Firsoff

Polish exile Firsoff was another post-war author. After suffering from shell-shock during the war, he convalesced at Achlean in Glen Feshie after several years in London, later met Perry, and accompanied him on hill walks. Firsoff's *The Cairngorms on Foot and Ski* (1949) differed from Perry's book. Firsoff did not fear the Cairngorms and admired them. A bold solo hill walker and ski-mountaineer, and occasionally rock-climber in company, he camped alone in the high hills, and wrote quite well about the area. He liked local folk. On one occasion he stayed at Luibeg Cottage with Bob and Helen Scott, and Bob had a good regard for him. Unfortunately his photograph of the cottage below the old pine-wood was printed the wrong way round. He knew the Polish mountains before the war and wrote a book about them, *The Tatra Mountains*, as well as *Ski Track on the Battlefield* and *The Unity of Europe*, and later a book about gemstones.

Nan Shepherd

An unusual variant was Nan Shepherd's *The Living Mountain* (1977). Some revere her book. It contains sensitive writing about how she felt about the Cairngorms in the 1930s, and also up to 1947 when she completed the manuscript but laid it aside. There are a few cases where she mentions events after 1947, the Ptarmigan Restaurant on Cairn Gorm, the supposed adverse effects on snow buntings, and the Feith Buidhe Disaster in November 1971, but these are insufficient to provide an up to date impression. Her book is firmly rooted in her personal experience of the area and a very few of its local indigenous folk.

(Readers may be interested to know of her book *In the Cairngorms – Poems,* Galileo Publishers, 2014. Originally published in 1934 by The Moray Press, it has now been re-issued with a Foreword by Robert Macfarlane, published by The Canons. Hamish Brown reviews it in the 2015 *Scottish Mountaineering Club Journal,* pp. 655–656, but much of his review consists of lavish praise for her book *The Living Mountain,* also recently reprinted in 2011 with an Introduction by Robert Macfarlane, published by The Canons. Brown's praise is exaggerated in my view. He wrote: 'She knew these mountains in every mood.' Readers can decide for themselves whether they agree with this claim, by looking at the many quotations from her book that I have made below. Referring to her poems in Scots, Macfarlane writes of this as her poems in the Doric, and Brown also uses the phrase in the Doric for some poems. In fact, use of the term Doric and even more so the absurd 'The Doric', when northern Scots is meant, signifies someone unwilling to use northern Scots in general conversation, but fancifully wishing to be seen to have some acquaintance with the indigenous language of north-east Scotland.

We schoolchildren born and brought up in north Aberdeenshire never used the term Doric, and I never heard it used by indigenous Scots speakers. It has sadly become a strange fashion, enjoying much publicity by those who should know better. It does not appear in the *Scottish National Dictionary*, and David Murison its life-long editor did not use it in conversation when I visited him twice after his retirement to Fraserburgh. Of relevance to Nan Shepherd is the fact that she did not use the absurd term Doric or The Doric in her books, and likewise in her conversation with us).

Always have I found her book fanciful, contrived, and fundamentally anthropocentric. Soon after its publication I read it once, and it meant little to me. I did not read it again until preparing this review. It is a good example of what some Aberdeen climbers in the 1950s called Salvationism, a way of gaining salvation for a person going to the hills or writing about them. They spoke the term with some sarcasm. The fanciful approach mirrored Nan's personality, as I experienced first hand. I knew her fairly well in 1961–77, and my wife Jenny knew her very well and was a good friend.

Nan knew of the deep interests of Jenny and me in the Cairngorms and of our long friendship with Carrie Nethersole-Thompson of Whitewell and other local folk mentioned in her book. Amazingly, her book ignores Carrie's husband Desmond Nethersole-Thompson, and their son Brock and daughter Myrtle, a family who lived in a little green corrugated-iron house below the old Whitewell croft where Carrie Mackenzie was raised and where her parents still lived when I first visited Desmond. A brilliant nest-finder in her own right, long before she met Desmond, Carrie had a strong desire to go to the high tops and did so alone, in years when it was generally regarded as odd for a woman to go to the hills. Desmond and she wrote several pioneering publications on bird behaviour, breeding and habitat, and Brock became a very good field observer, contributing many notes for his father's books. Nan ignored all this.

In the book, she praised James Downie's nephew Jim MacGregor, who lived at Tomintoul, a high croft above Braemar. She never mentioned that he was a well known postman in the late 1940s and early 1950s. His nickname in Braemar was 'The Creeper'. A friendly but somewhat dull character, he showed no interest in going to the hills.

Braemar's outstanding hill-walker in the late 1930s and up to 1945, who remained a resident many years thereafter, was Miss Mary Farquharson. Everyone in Braemar and district knew Mary, a popular figure. She was local indigenous hill walker par excellence, in a way that fitted nobody else on the Spey or Dee sides of the Cairngorms before the 1930s or for several decades since. Nan's book contains not a word about her.

Likewise, Nan did not mention at Luibeg the well known brothers Donald and Sandy Macdonald and their sister Nell (all nicknamed Bynack, as e.g. Donald Bynack, for having been raised at Bynack Lodge), or the later James Beattie and Miss George there, or that exceptionally knowledgeable hill-man Ian Grant of Inverey. Jenny and I knew that Nan was a snob, but this dearth of names at Braemar and the relatively large amount of space given to a very select few at Whitewell and Aviemore imply that she seldom visited Mar, did not know the Braemar area or its folk well, and even at Whitewell ignored the exceptional Nethersole-Thompsons.

Nan never raised these matters with Jenny or me, and if we raised them she soon changed the subject. Though Editor of the *Aberdeen University Review* for many years, she found it very hard to get her own writing published. However, she was well known to Aberdeen journalists such as Cuthbert Graham and to Aberdeen publishers. Had this not been so, it is unlikely that *The Living Mountain* would have been published. Jenny spent much time with Nan over a novel that Nan had written, and eventually typed the manuscript as a favour to her. However, Jenny found the story dull, complex, and poorly told. The publishers whom Nan approached refused it at that time.

A snob towards most working-class folk, she was nevertheless a hospitable old lady to her close friends, including Mrs Sheila Clouston of Banchory and Jenny, and in later years she diligently cared for Maimie her housekeeper when Maimie fell ill. *The Living Mountain* reveals her sensitive nature, especially her sense of touch.

I now give some quotations from that book, along

with some comments. Comment is unnecessary in certain cases where the error is clearly evident.

Title *The Living Mountain* and sub-title *A Celebration of the Cairngorm Mountains of Scotland*. Unlike indigenous rural folk in Ireland, indigenous Scots in the Cairngorms region and elsewhere in north-east Scotland and the central Highlands do not use the terms 'mountain' or 'mountains' for Scottish hills. These terms are used in this sense only by in-comers, signifying their lack of respect for local tradition and tongue.

In Nan's Foreword on p. vi, (referring to the Feith Buidhe Disaster in 1971), a group of schoolchildren, belated, fail to find the hut where they should have spent the night. They shelter against a wall of snow, but in the morning, in spite of the heroic efforts of their instructress, only she and one boy are alive. (Most of this is incorrect. They were belated only because they started too late. The instructress decided to stop and bivouac only a short distance from the hut, even though weather conditions were still not bad and some daylight remained. They did not shelter against a wall of snow. The instructress chose a dangerous spot to bivouac and gave the children instructions that could scarcely have been worse.).

p. vi, A restaurant hums on the heights and between it and the summit of Cairn Gorm grows scruffy, the very heather tatty from the scrape of boots (no heather grew between the Ptarmigan Restaurant and the top of Cairn Gorm, because the altitude is too high).

Her continual use of 'mountain' is alien, as is her anglicised 'valley' as in Slugain valley, p.18 Einich valley, and p.19 Ey valley, instead of glen.

p. 5, To pit oneself against the mountain is necessary for every climber....Granite, of which the Cairngorms are built, weathers too smoothly and squarely to make the best conditions for rock-climbing....The Guide Book and the *Cairngorm Club Journal* give the attested climbs (all but the last phrase is incorrect and misleading, and climbs since 1950 have been described in the Scottish Mountaineering Club's *Climbers' Guide* and in the *Scottish Mountaineering Club Journal*).

p. 11, my companion was a rabid naturalist.

She mangled many Gaelic place names, such as Ben a' Bhuird, Beinnie Coire, Ben Ouran, Loch Dubh, Dubh Loch at Beinn Mheadhoin, Dubh Loch at Beinn a' Bhuird, Loch an Uaine, and Monadhliaths. Her map gives the anglicised Green Loch instead of Lochan Uaine, and shows Whitewell south of Loch an Eilein.

p. 12, grim bastions.

p. 13, higher up the loch (Avon) there is no way out, save by scrambling up one or other of the burns that tumble from the heights: except that, above the Shelter Stone, a gap opens between the hills to Loch Etchachan, and here the scramble up is shorter.

p. 19, I have seen, in intense still summer heat, not only the corries but the whole plateau burning with a hot violet incandescence until noon. Sunset also lights the corries, but this must be seen on the other (Spey) side.

p. 23, the Wells of Dee. It wells from the rock, and flows away (It does not well from the rock, but from groundwater in gravel and shattered boulder-fields above the rock).

p. 23, the Lairig Ghru, is so sheer and narrow that when mists roll among the precipices, lifting and settling again, it is sometimes hard to tell whether a glimpse of rock wall belongs to the mountain on which one is standing or to another across the cleft.

p. 23, High on the Ben MacDhui side, though 300 feet lower than the wells on Braeriach, two waters begin a mere step from one another. One runs east, falls over the precipice into Loch Avon and turns north to the Spey; the other, starting westwards, slips over the edge as the March Burn and falls into the Lairig Ghru. (The wells are more than 200 m apart, and do not start 300 feet lower than the wells on Braeriach).

p. 24, I can think of no good reason for trudging through the oppressive Lairig Ghru, except to see them (Pools of Dee)....The Cairngorm water is all clear. Flowing from granite, with no peat to darken it, it has never the golden amber....so often praised in Highland burns.

p. 25, Two of the lochs are black by name – the Dubh Loch of Ben a' Bhuird and the Dubh Loch that lies in the cleft that cuts the plateau, the Little Lairig, but they are black by place and not by nature, shadowed heavily by rock. That the water has no darkness in it is plain when one remembers that the clear green Quoich rises out of the one loch and the Avon is fed by the other. (In fact, it is the Dubh Lochan, not the Dubh Loch, on Beinn (not Ben) a' Bhuird, and further down are the smaller Dubh Lochain, plural. None of them is shadowed heavily by rock, save in winter. All look dark because of a dark substrate. It is the Dubh Lochan, plural, in the Lairig an Laoigh or Little Lairig, they are not shadowed heavily by rock but are open to the south, and are peaty. Quoich Water appears green in its lower reaches where it flows over mica schist, but not higher up. It rises high on Cnap a' Chleirich, not in the Dubh Lochan).

p. 26, the most appalling quality of water is its strength.

p. 29, The freezing of running water is another mystery. The strong white stuff....is itself held and punished.

p. 29, the tracks of birds and animals.

p. 30, (of tracks in winter snow), a fox dragging his brush (a fox does not drag its brush), grouse thick-footed, plover thin (no plover are there in deep January snow).... Since then I have watched many burns in the process of freezing (and prolonged description follows, but nowhere does she describe the formation of grue by ice spangles freezing at the bottom and rising to the surface, which shows that either she spent very little time watching freezing burns or was a poor observer).

p. 31, Loose snow blown in the sun looks like the ripples running through corn (blown snow moving in sunshine does not resemble ripples of wind through cereal. crops)....snow on a furious gale freezes on the sheltered sides of stones on a hilltop in long crystals. I have seen these converge slightly as the wind blows round both sides of the stones. (Frozen long crystals are due not to snow but to fog freezing, and form on the windward side, not the leeward sheltered side. Seton Gordon aptly referred to them as fog crystals. Her account of seeing them converge is fanciful imagination).

p. 33, the January blizzards, thick, close and wild – the *blin' drift* that shuts a man into deadly isolation. To go into such conditions on the mountains is folly; the gamekeeper's dictum is: if you can't see your own footsteps behind you in the snow, don't go on.

p. 33, But a blizzard may blow up so rapidly that one is caught (incorrect, for the sky always shows early signs of impending prolonged snowfall, hours before it arrives).

p. 34, even in July there were solid walls of snow, many feet thick and as high as the corrie precipices, leaning outwards from the rock and following its contours (absurd exaggeration).

p. 34, blizzard is the most deadly condition of these hills. It is wind that is to be feared, even more than snow itself.

In places the exaggerations appear ludicrous and nonsensical to those with deep experience of the area, for example on p. 39. 'This is part of the horror of walking in mist on the plateau', and p. 40 'when the mist thickens, one walks in a blind world. And that is bad: though there is a thrill in its eeriness, and a sound satisfaction in not getting lost. For not getting lost is a matter of the mind – of keeping one's head, of having map and compass and knowing how to use them, of staying steady'.

p. 41, For even in a night that has neither moon nor stars the mountains can still be seen. The sky cannot be wholly dark. In the most overcast night it is much lighter than the earth. (She could not have been out in a really dark night).

p. 46, it is on only some of the summer days that insects can fly to the mountain top.

p. 47, Bog myrtle is the mountain exampler (bog myrtle grows on lower moorland).

p. 49 The very sites of these ancient sawmills are forgotten.

p. 50, (of resinous pine roots), *rossitty reets* (we call them that on the Aberdeenshire side of the hill). (Jenny and I never heard Nan speak north-east Scots, even though we often used it in her company).

p. 55, Birds, animals, insects.

p. 56, Mr Seton Gordon claims that Golden Eagle rises from her eyrie clumsily, especially when the air is calm. I have never had, I was going to say the luck, but I should say rather the assiduity and patience to see an eagle rising from the eyrie, but I have watched one fly out from the vicinity of an eyrie, alight in heather some distance away, rise again and again alight, and there was nothing noteworthy in its movement (why recount an anecdotal observation by an inexperienced observer and somehow imply questioning of an undoubtedly experienced one?).

p. 56, the wind tears across these desolate marches.

p. 59, the snow buntings....have a delicate perfection that is enhanced by the savagery of their home. Sit quietly for a while in some of the loneliest and most desolate crannies of the mountain, where the imagination is overpowered by grim bastions of the rock.

p. 69, Man....has driven the snow bunting from its nesting-sites.

p. 72, (of local folk), They have only condemnation for winter climbing. They know how terrific the force of a hurricane can be on the plateau and they speak with bitter realism of the young fools who trifle with human life by disregarding the warnings they are given (I never met a local person who had experienced a hurricane on the plateau, and extremely few who had been on the plateau in winter, even on fine days).

P. 80, the next quotation describes how she awoke at the edge of Coire Bhrochain, and runs, but to that first horrified state, dissociated from all thought and all memory, sensation purely, the drop seemed inordinate. With a gasp of relief I said 'Coire Brochain', turned round on my back, eased myself from the edge, and sat up. I had looked into the abyss.

p. 82, Out of sleep too I have heard the roaring of stags; but these are no longer outdoor nights. The nights then are cold and dark, and the roaring is fearsome as it comes from the hills that are usually so silent....after many days of rain, I have waked to hear the burns come down in spate, with a duller and more persistent roar than that of the stags, but in its own way as fearsome.

p. 87, The lochan below Loch Dubh seems enormous; the steep climb beyond it towers upward so giddily into nothingness that I am assailed by fear: this must be the precipice itself that I am climbing – the lochan was the loch. I have passed it and am clambering towards the cliff. I know it can't be true, but the dim white ghostliness out of which stark shapes batter at my brain has overpowered my reason....I scramble downwards, and the grey, rather dismal, normality below the mist has a glow of comfort.

p. 90, This plunge into the cold water of a mountain pool seems for a brief moment to disintegrate the very self; it is not to be borne: One is lost, stricken, annihilated. Then life pours back.

Seton Gordon never wrote such nonsense, and in my experience and that of others who knew him well and discussed this with me, he never spoke it.

Chapter 3. Deerstalking, deer fences and walkers

In a review paper on 'The wildlife potential of the Cairngorms region', published in *Scottish Birds* of 1977, I discussed briefly the conflict between hill-walking and deerstalking. I wrote, 'Hikers have long been unpopular on grouse moors and deer forests, as their disturbance is said to reduce bags of Red Grouse and spoil deer stalks....As for Red Deer, again there is no good evidence of damage. Hikers are sometimes seen to disturb stags which are being stalked, and so ruin the stalk. However, there are occasions when stags, disturbed by hikers not seen by the stalkers, run within rifle range from outside and get shot. The loss of shots due to observed hikers must be weighed against the extra shots due to disturbance by hikers who have not been seen by the stalking party' (Watson 1977a).

R.J. Wheater (1977) later contested this with a letter published in *Scottish Birds*, writing, 'I am surprised that Dr Watson, who is rightly acknowledged as a highly competent field naturalist, believes that stalkers would normally take stags that arrive at the gun having been disturbed by hikers or others'.

I replied, 'I have seen about 350 stags shot. Most were stalked at leisure. Several of these were missed because of disturbance by hikers in the course of the stalk, but several were killed that appeared on the move without having been stalked at leisure' (Watson 1977b).

Of course, stalkers like to choose a stag at leisure and then shoot it after a stalk, which cannot be done if they have hurriedly to shoot a stag that appears suddenly. So, disturbance by hikers undoubtedly affects the quality of the stag shooting, but cannot reduce the number of stags shot. David Bates, the editor of *Scottish Birds*, had published my 1977 paper and the subsequent correspondence by Wheater and me.

David Bates told me that Lord Dulverton, then owner of Glenfeshie Estate, had put Wheater up to writing a letter criticising my paper. After David accepted Wheater's letter and my reply to be published alongside it, Wheater wrote to him asking to withdraw his letter, but David replied that this would be possible only if I agreed, and I did not.

Astonishingly, Dulverton then sent a letter to David Bates, demanding that he withdraw the Wheater letter, which David rightly refused to do. Subsequently, Lt Col. J.P. Grant of Rothiemurchus Estate sent a letter complaining about my paper, not to *Scottish Birds* but to the landowners' journal *Landowning in Scotland*. I had suggested that the best parts of the Cairngorms region for wildlife and landscape should be owned by the state, to give long-term continuity of management. This of course is typical for national parks and other outstanding areas for landscape and wildlife in many countries. In an article published in *Landowning in Scotland*, Grant (!978) asserted that I had advocated land nationalisation. I had not done so.

Another statement that he disliked was that I had mentioned illegal persecution of protected raptors on some private estates in the Cairngorms region. This was fact, but he wrote that he on Rothiemurchus Estate and Lord Dulverton on the neighbouring Glen Feshie Estate protected raptors. I replied with a letter published in *Landowning in Scotland*, pointing out that I had not called for land nationalisation and had not named either him or Lord Dulverton, or their estates (Watson 1979a).

Grant and Dulverton followed this with individual letters to *Landowning in Scotland*, which were duly published (Grant 1979a; Dulverton 1979). Following my factual statements about illegal persecution of protected raptors by gamekeepers on some estates in the Cairngorms region, Grant asserted of me that 'his sweeping and unqualified accusation is biased, unfair and possibly even libellous to those keepers whose efforts contribute materially to wildlife conservation'.

Grant then wrote to the Chairman of the Natural Environment Council, Professor J.W.L. Beament, complaining about my paper. The Chairman asked John Jeffers, Director of the Institute of Terrestrial Ecology, whether my paper had been seen in draft by a senior officer of ITE. In fact, it had been read carefully and cleared for sending to *Scottish Birds* by Dr Jack Dempster, the scientist in charge of animal research in ITE. Satisfied by this, the Chairman wrote a letter to Grant, stating that he and NERC would take no action. Dulverton then put further pressure on the Chairman. Sadly, the Chairman dropped his integrity by changing his mind and kowtowing to Dulverton. He then sent a letter to *Landowning in Scotland*, dissociating NERC from the comments about landowners in my paper (Beament 1979). This was disgraceful, given his earlier agreement to take no action once he knew that my paper in draft form had been subject to review by ITE. John Jeffers, a man of integrity, earned my deep respect by refusing to kow-tow, and wrote to me, standing by me and regretting the Chairman's move and change of mind without evidence. Below Beament's letter in *Landowning in Scotland* appeared a brief letter by Grant (1979b), stating that he was grateful for Beament's letter.

Astonishingly, R.J. Wheater later became Vice-Chairman of Scottish Natural Heritage and was on a short leet of three for the Chairmanship. This tells much about the Scottish Office's choice of people for the boards of the quangos that it ran. For some years later, Dulverton was the NERC representative on the Red Deer Commission, an inappropriate non-scientist representative to a quango Commission that was already dominated by landowners of deer-forests. The Secretary to NERC, eminent fishery biologist Ray Beverton, told us at the Institute of Terrestrial Ecology at its Banchory station that Dulverton had asked to be NERC representative. What is worse was that NERC agreed.

Here is an unusual response to deer fences and access to walkers. One afternoon in September 1990, Tom Weir and I after a hill walk went for a cup of tea to a cafe below the Campsies, and spoke to two men having afternoon tea. Tweed-suited and with woollen ties and walking boots, they carried old rucksacks and wooden walking sticks, and wore tweed bonnets. In looks and speech they seemed archetypal retired gents, utterly genteel and in respect of the law. When Tom and I bemoaned the deer fences that were cutting off access on the Camspies, they smiled and said "That's no bother to us. We go where we like". One of them fished out from his rucksack a pair of wire-cutters and held it up triumphantly in front of our faces, with a gleam in his eye, before quickly putting it out of sight again!

On a later visit to the Campsies, this time as a board member of the Countryside Commission for Scotland, I was on a bus tour with the board and senior officers, along with English and Welsh board members of the Countryside Commission and their senior officers, and board members and senior officers of the Nature Conservancy Council for Scotland. The bus stopped on the Stirling side of the Campsies, in a glen that had been ploughed up and planted with dense conifers, enclosed by tall deer fences with wire netting. After a CCS officer described what had happened, I condemned the Forestry Commission for pursuing what I called official vandalism to land, paid with taxpayers' money. Magnus Magnusson, then Chairman of NCC Scotland, said eloquently but ridiculously, "I'm with Adam on this one. I would gladly go into the ditch with him and face the bulldozers!" Just before this, I had publicly criticised him over his unacceptable undemocratic behaviour about the choice of membership of the Cairngorms Working Party and I had called for heads to roll. At the site visit to the Campsies, I responded to his appeal by saying "I didn't say I'd go into the ditch, but I'd be willing to push you in!" As the many who were present laughed openly, Magnusson had the sense to smile and we then made our way to the bus. I think those present will have remembered the issue of fences and access better from these five minutes than hours of detailed discussion!

In the website *winterhighland*, Helen Rennie described her ski-tour on low hills near Inverness in early 2010. She crossed young trees on deep snow, but once trees have reach two metres or higher they prevent access except on rides and roads. Plantations have removed huge areas of moorland and farmland that gave good skiing near towns. Many farmers have ploughed up moorland and also old tracks that were rights of way, except unusually where a farmer decided to keep the old track and respected local tradition and the right of way. Even the two tweedy old gents could hardly defeat bulldozer and plough. You can't stay in the ditch all the time!

Chapter 4. Professor Vero Copner Wynne-Edwards, 1906–97, a personal sketch by Adam Watson

(from The Ratcatcher, early 1997), a newsletter run by and for those at the former research station of the Institute of Terrestrial Ecology at Hill of Brathens, Banchory

V.C. Wynne-Edwards died on 5 January 1997 at Inchmarlo nursing home, where he and his wife Jeannie, in poor health, had moved from Torphins in spring 1996.

I first met him at Marischal College in December 1946. He was 40, Professor; I was 16, at Turriff school in Buchan. George Waterston, the first professional ornithologist to work in the area, had been based at Huntly in 1944–45, studying wood pigeons and rooks, and I gave him much help with nest-recording, counting and other fieldwork. He hoped to start the Scottish Ornithologists Club and had me lined up as a founder of an Aberdeen Branch. When well-known ornithologist Wynne-Edwards was appointed Professor of Natural History at Aberdeen, hopes for a new SOC rose.

I went to Aberdeen to see him. He treated me as an adult and said he hoped to form an Aberdeen Branch with my help. George had told him of my bird observations, notes in *British Birds,* and interest in the Cairngorms and in snow. Although there was an aloofness about him, we had instant rapport through many mutual interests. My diary records laconically 'he is quite a nice chap'!

In 1947 we went on some weekend days to the Cairngorms and Ythan estuary. An all-round naturalist, zoologist and botanist, he had a great knowledge of different species, the world literature and its practitioners. We went by rail to Edinburgh for talks on a new SOC and new *Scottish Naturalist.* On a second Edinburgh trip he took me to the International Ornithological Congress and introduced me to many delegates. To go to both meetings I had to get off school. The headmaster agreed willingly, when someone told him that the AW in *The Scotsman*, author of paid *Nature Notes* on the Cairngorms and Deveron, was me, not my father of the same name!

Returning from the IOC, we stopped to walk up Glas Maol. A strong walker, he said most people were slow, but he liked going with me as I could already outpace him on steep rough ground and snow, and was gaining rapidly in stamina. In later years he became too keen for my liking on checking his times, and showed impatience if I stopped for long to watch something of interest, even though I could now far outpace him if I chose to. Desmond Nethersole-Thompson classified ornithologists as "arsers" and "leggers", he being a 100% arser. I think it best to be both, for studying numbers and behaviour of birds at low density on the hill. To DNT, VCWE was a 100% legger. Despite hundreds of summer walks on the Cairngorms and Mounth, VCWE told me in the mid 1970s he still had not seen a dotterel nest. One must be a part arser to see many dotterel nests, and a part legger to study dotterel numbers.

My solicitor father wished me to follow in his firm but the law didn't interest me. When George Waterston in 1944 said there would be ecological jobs after the war and my observations would suit me for one of them, my father was sceptical. When VCWE with his quiet authority said so, he believed him.

We began the SOC Aberdeen Branch while I was at school. He was Chairman; I was Secretary, in at the deep end. I made mistakes, as I had no model to follow. I soon learned that he expected me to pick up experience myself, the hard way. Maybe it was the best way, though at times I wondered what I had let myself in for at that shy young age.

In 1948 I became a science student at Aberdeen. In December Tom Weir and I spent a week at Luibeg, climbing and skiing. VCWE came up for a night. Next morning, thick ice from a severe frost sealed most of the burn. Tom and I, shivering at dawn, in amazement saw a naked VCWE break the ice with his feet before plunging into a deep pool! On a superb morning he accompanied us up Glen Geusachan to the Moine Mhor. There we parted, he to go by Glen Feshie to catch a train to a Pitlochry meeting. He carried committee papers in his pack on that long hill walk!

The University was still small, and stimulating as a

result.. In the Department the third-year and honours students had tea standing in the same tiny room as the staff. There were some great discussions, as well as a stress on succinct writing and criticism. VCWE led the way on criticism, and in the *Scottish Naturalist* had a scathing review of Frank Fraser Darling's *Natural History in the Highlands and Islands*. The famed editors and Darling were furious and defensive. Yet the book was careless, and incorrect on some important points. Sadly, this rebuff from the natural history establishment made him chary, and he never wrote such a critical review again.

Lecturer Robert Carrick could enthuse students in a way that the more introvert VCWE lacked. Helped by them, he blocked every starling nest hole in Torphins and substituted boxes where he could mark and weigh chicks. He asked me to help him photograph eagles on several weekends, by showing him eyries and helping erect hides. In the bothy morning and night, and noon when it rained, my eagle observations excited him, almost as if it were his own study. He suggested certain aspects to stress for my honours thesis.

When I returned to Aberdeen, lit up with enthusiasm, it was the only time I saw VCWE suggest a different idea. Although not refusing the eagle idea, he suggested building on my ptarmigan observations. He said this would be of more general interest, the bird's winter ecology and population dynamics were almost unknown, it abounded in the Cairngorms, and my experience and enjoyment of solo ski-mountaineering would make study possible even in storms. In the end I did study ptarmigan on Derry Cairngorm, and he was right that ptarmigan problems have more general biological relevance.

It was in the honours year that I learned another aspect of VCWE. He gave no supervision or training to his students, honours, MSc or PhD. It was sink or swim. Later he said the best research was done by picking the right people and letting them get on with it the way they wanted to do it. With hindsight, I believe this may be appropriate for later work, but every student benefits from critical discussion of thinking, fieldwork and writing. Certainly he would have had no time for today's smothering of scientific imagination by pedestrian funding agents with more money than sense, who long ago lost the ability to think critically if they ever even had it in the first place.

In 1952 I won a post-graduate scholarship with the Arctic Institute of North America at McGill University, Montreal. AINA Director Patrick Baird asked me to be zoologist on a big expedition to Baffin Island in 1953. In that summer VCWE went on his own expedition to the east Baffin coast to study gulls. He joined the end of our expedition and helped carry our equipment out through difficult glaciated terrain among some of the world's most spectacular mountains. In that international company he was relaxed as I never saw before or since. It seemed right for all of us to call him Vero. He enjoyed the Swiss glaciologists' alpine songs. His aloofness vanished, but returned on the ice-breaker as we came into the St Lawrence. Years after, he remembered the songs, and when singing them with me at my wedding party came close to relaxing almost like Baffin days again.

When I was assistant lecturer in the Department on return from Montreal, David Lack spoke to the Biological Society on animal population regulation, about the time of his book (1954). A good speaker, he summarised the view that animals breed as fast as they can, and that density-dependent mortality regulated numbers, usually through food shortage, with dominance behaviour determining which individuals would die but not the eventual number that would breed. Sitting beside me, VCWE whispered excitedly in my ear "He's ignoring slow-breeding seabirds and elephants, but I daren't ask a question in case he steals my ideas. I'll have to publish mine first". Shortly afterwards he sent a paper to *Ibis* on slow-breeding seabirds, but the Oxford establishment turned it down. That made him decide to begin writing *Animal Dispersion in relation to Social Behaviour* (1962).

He was an early appointee to the Nature Conservancy board. The NC declared the Cairngorms Nature Reserve in 1954, and a new warden and rules irritated the indigenous deer stalkers. Famed among them was Bob Scott, to whom the Derry beat of Mar was his personal kingdom in a way that no laird owning such an area could emulate. Bob's instant sarcastic humour was legendary, and I have never seen pompous patronising Admiral or Sheriff silenced so effectively. Once when my father was staying at Luibeg with Bob, they walked across to the nearby Derry Lodge in the evening when the NC committee was there. VCWE produced a big dram. Bob, in good form even when sober, soon let fly with virulent complaints about the NC. Hoping to defuse this, VCWE joked "Well Bob, we'll just have to have you on the Conservancy committee to put your ideas into practice"! Quick as a flash, Bob retorted "I widna fyle ma sheen waalkin aside the buggers"! (I would not befoul (usually with excrement) my shoes walking beside the buggers)!

About that time, VCWE twice came climbing with me on the red granite sea-cliffs of Longhaven. Although he had done little climbing and was now 50, he seconded me on exposed routes with confidence. He would have been a natural mountaineer had he started earlier.

When the Scottish Landowners Federation in 1956 wished to fund research on red grouse and did not persuade the NC to do the job, VCWE offered his Department. In 1957 I joined David Jenkins at Glen Esk, both as Senior Research Fellows in the Department. Some lairds on the big Grouse Liaison Committee wanted us to do *ad hoc* work on their ideas, with almost as many suggestions as lairds at the table. Of course we thought this approach useless, but they had the cash and could have insisted. Fortunately they accepted VCWE's verdict, with his usual grave authority, that we must be allowed to do it our way. In the end, not one idea suggested by them proved the remedy for the low grouse stocks that worried them.

During these years, and later when Honorary Director of the Nature Conservancy Grouse & Moorland Ecology Unit in the 1960s, he never suggested we drop one line and substitute another to his liking. His book *Group Selection and Evolution,* which stressed our study, might imply that he had a more active personal role. In fact, his role was one of enabling work to start and shielding us from interference. This was more important than the active role which he could have taken had he so wished.

Only once did he insist on an active role, when *The New Scientist* asked him for an article. He could have written a general review, but wanted to use our data showing that heather shoot length on different areas was related to grouse breeding success in the same year. I was unhappy as it was only the first year of data on shoots, but he saw it as confirming his ideas and put it in the article. When year 2 came, there was no sign of the correlation!

A failing was that when someone under his wing behaved unacceptably to another, he would hear all sides and then shirk taking decisive action. I was therefore unsurprised to learn later that, when NERC Chairman, he failed to curb destructive empire builders. He was a very good enabler, not a very good leader.

A VCWE characteristic in later decades (though not in his early years at Aberdeen) was overstated praise of Highland lairds. DNT and I had to tone down this in his draft Preface to our book *The Cairngorms,* as it would have been incongruous in a factual book. Although VCWE disliked some changes that adversely affected Scottish hills and woods, he did not put his head above the parapet on such conservation conflicts. However, his signing of *A Blueprint of Survival* in 1972 (which criticised government environmental policies) was a notable exception that may have cost him the knighthood he sought.

He was a bold cross-country skier, but the risks of going alone made him slightly chary, and sometimes he tagged on to me, as I had far more experience. Usually this was fine, but twice his attitude alienated the party. In February 1965 he accompanied Mike Taylor and me from Glen Lui to Beinn a' Bhuird. My father skied so far and said he would drive the car round to meet us at Invercauld. Mike had with him an experienced walker who was a learner on skis. All went well until we came to the steep south corries in poor light under fog and light falling snow. I led the way down the best route, with excellent conditions for turning, but Mike's friend was slow and we waited for him often. Nothing is worse for a learner's morale than seeing everybody far away in front.

At the first trees I halted to wait. We were now safely off the mountain, but still had miles to go. Impatient, VCWE suddenly took off and disappeared. I led the way across to Gleann an t-Slugain and down it in failing light. On the path in the lower glen I was relieved to see his ski tracks. I knew he must have gone further east and was concerned he might come to grief in the rocky glacial meltwater channels there. In near darkness we came to my father's car with its cheery lights and roaring stove, and were plied with hot soup and tea beside a rather grumpy VCWE. Later, my father told me his first words to him were "I'm afraid there's a slow member in the party, and I've a roast at home!" To us it was wrong to quit at dusk without a word, and to leave the slowest member.

In April 1965, Tom Weir, his wife Rhona, my father and I were to ski to Ben Macdui, when we halted to take a photograph. VCWE stopped his car and said he would like to join us. Tom told us he was recovering from flu and would be slow, but would manage to reach Ben Macdui. On the way up Glen Lui he was glad to see his first wheatear of the year, but VCWE's impatience cut this short. Later, Tom and I were ascending Ben Macdui slowly but steadily, having good conversations, when VCWE, who had been well ahead all the way up the Sron Riach, skied down, sending snow flying towards us as he skidded flamboyantly to a stop. Remarking on the party's slow progress, he said dinner awaited him at home. He took the edge off what would otherwise have been a perfect day for the rest of us.

As scientist he was remarkably defensive about his ideas. He gave me the page proofs of his first book, but that stage was too late for me to do more than note printers' errors. Before it was published he gave a seminar on his ideas, at the Department. In the course of this he described the spectacular, wheeling, pre-roost flights of starlings as "epideictic behaviour", by which, he said, they assessed their own numbers in relation to the food supply. One or two in the audience tentatively asked innocuous questions. Then, In his down-to-earth Aberdonian fashion, Sandy Anderson said it sounded doubtful. VCWE's face showed instant anger, and he later told George Dunnet and me of his great annoyance that the professor's ideas were criticised in front of the students, and his hope that nothing like this would ever happen again.

The book raised much controversy, and Elton, Lack and others castigated it in reviews. The Edward Grey Institute conference had an electric atmosphere at New Year 1963, because he gave the main talk and his book came under fire. He said that animal populations show self-restraint in breeding and use of food, and that the social behaviour which controls this has evolved by group selection, over-riding Darwinian individual selection. Against this, Lack and others argued strongly that rapid breeding through individual selection would lead to these genotypes preponderating at the expense of any that involved self-restraint.

The row over his first book led to frosty relations with Lack. When Lack visited Blackhall to see the grouse team while preparing his book *Population Studies in Birds,* he said he would like to break the ice with VCWE and asked me to help. I approached VCWE, who agreed to a trip with Lack and family, and me.

As I drove up Glen Quoich in July 1968, David showed his good fieldcraft by spotting a wryneck motionless on a pine branch. Later we walked for miles over plateau and corries seeking the rare brook saxifrage, without success. At lunch we sat by a mossy spring, admiring the view. David tentatively mentioned population regulation, and Wynne tentatively replied. The discussion then ended as David spotted nine hen dotterel beside us. He certainly was showing his prowess as an observer.

We then spread out for another plant search, walking slowly, but VCWE announced that he had not had enough exercise and would run down the hill and see us in the glen. The Lacks and I continued searching, and eventually found the brook saxifrage in flower on a cold cliff. Elation! Later, when we picked up Wynne, hot and sticky after running in the sun, a beaming David told him we had found the plant! It was a moment of supreme one-upmanship, which had its funny side to VCWE too, after his brief initial disappointment. More importantly, the ice was now well and truly broken.

In those years he was on many committees. After Bob Robel from Kansas gave a Culterty seminar, I was with DNT outside when VCWE came out to his car. I told VCWE I would like his support in applying to fund work on radio-telemetry in grouse. Desmond regaled us years later with this, as VCWE looked agitated, checked his diary, and said "I've just realised I'm supposed to be at a committee meeting in Pitlochry at this very moment. How much money do you want -- a thousand, two thousand or what"? Desmond was amazed at my honesty in naming a modest sum. He thought if I had said £4000 I would have got it on the nod!

After David Jenkins became NC Director of Research (Scotland) at Edinburgh, he wished to end the grouse study that he had helped begin. I said I would resign and take offers from North America to go there with any I chose from the grouse team. VCWE at once backed our work, and said if NC ended it he'd have us in a special research group in the University. He meant every word. Again this did the trick.

In the late 1960s he wrote an article and gave me

a draft in case he had made factual errors on grouse. I corrected them as usual, but this time went further and used my red pen fairly freely. I recall a strained meeting when he thanked me for correcting the errors but disapproved of my other comments. He accepted that hypothesis testing and issues of confirmation versus refutation were useful in research, but said unlike most scientists he tended to think globally about animals and literature, and so could not be fettered by the usual rules.

This made me think it was as well that not many scientists were like him, but it was maybe good that occasionally there were one or two to make the rest of us sit up. There have been heretical past views which later became accepted. That may happen yet for group selection. However, the main flaw in his books was that he pushed some findings, such as our grouse work, too far and much too one-sidedly, at the expense of other explanations.

Another VCWE feature was unwillingness to accept new observations if they did not easily fit his view of the world. When I found evidence that grouse eggs varied in quality between populations and that some year classes of territorial grouse survived better than others, he showed total disbelief at first. When I showed at a seminar at Blackhall that fertilizer on heather failed to stop a cyclic grouse decline, he responded that it was merely one experiment that didn't work. Robert Moss then added that our prior prediction of the outcome increased the experiment's rigour, and he was right, but this cut no ice with VCWE. In 1977 I told him that for the first time in Scotland I had seen many berries of bog whortleberry *(Vaccinium uliginosum)*. He said I must be mistaken, as neither he nor Mrs Somerville (Botany Department recorder) had ever seen any. He believed it only when I showed him fresh twigs with berries a weekend later.

My wife and I used to drop in unannounced to see him and Jeannie. While having tea on one of these occasions he asked if I had seen E.O. Wilson's new book *Sociobiology – the New Synthesis.* I was astonished when he added with a touch of envy "He's done it all now. There's nothing important left to study!"

In several such ways he differed greatly from most scientists. Each of the hundreds who came to see us from many countries wished to see the hill, the birds' behaviour, and other field work, but such details interested VCWE not. He liked going to the hills on foot and on ski with me, but not in particular to see our study areas or work on them.

Similarly he showed surprising inattention to detail and rigour on the few occasions when he did write about field topics after the 1950s. An example was when he stated (1964, *Advancement of Science* 21, 37–43, Multi-purpose land use and conservation in the Highlands) that the 200-acre dome of Cairn Gorm appeared to have been totally forsaken by all forms of vertebrate wildlife. He gave no evidence for this anecdotal claim, and indeed ptarmigan were at far higher density than usual. Later I had to reject the claim, in a paper about human impact on vertebrates there (1979, *Journal of Applied Ecology).* He therefore showed an interesting contrast whereby he was brilliant at seeing possibilities for other field workers and enabling them to do the work, but fairly uncritical when it came to observations in the field by himself. Charles Elton, in criticising VCWE's 1962 book in a review in *Nature,* stated that the main flaws stemmed from Wynne-Edwards' relative lack of experience of intensive field research.

When giving a talk on his ideas he read from a text, and pled by advocacy to an audience rather than by sharing with fellow workers. At the British Ecological Society's 1969 conference in Aberdeen he gave the last talk. As he ended with an exhortation, Mick (H.N.) Southern, sitting beside me, shook his head and groaned "Oh, Wynne!" despairingly, thinking his friend had again gone too far.

When writing the second book he had retired and was often at Torphins. Once when my wife and I called to see him and Jeannie, he told me in great excitement that he had just found out about the negative binomial distribution. He said it fitted the distances moved by ringed grouse that were later recovered dead. Along with the far greater distances moved by some hens, this was clear proof, he claimed, of group selection operating in the grouse. I replied that the negative binomial is merely a mathematical description of the distribution of certain phenomena, including incomes in the USA and other features that have nothing to do with animal populations and evolution. My wife recalls the stiff atmosphere while we had tea, relieved by Jeannie's unfailing friendliness and hospitality. Fortunately on this occasion he must have had second thoughts, as his book did not include this notion about the negative binomial.

For that book he returned to group selection, following work by Wade and others in the US. He said he had found the answer to the critics of his 1962 book. Fearing that others might hear of this new idea and publish it before him, he typed the book himself. He took the typescript to Brathens to see me, as he had made our grouse work central to his case for group selection and planned to have a cover showing a red grouse, which he described as "the golden bird". When he said "there are two people I fear when the book comes out, you and Maynard Smith", I replied that he should show the draft to Smith and me now, before the book was published. Though wanting me to correct factual errors, he left with the typescript under his arm after dithering for an hour. He did not show it to Prof Maynard Smith either. When asked to review the book for the *Journal of Animal Ecology*, I could not find any new idea that answered his earlier critics. I then asked him what it was, and he showed me the sentence. It did not answer his earlier critics.

Nevertheless one might ponder how many folk in their 60s, let alone 80s, are still working hard on academic projects, and still talking animatedly about natural history, science, snow, skiing, the Cairngorms, the Arctic, seabirds, the ptarmigan he was seeing on Morven, the flowers and other plants he had noticed recently, and so on. He was a naturalist with a great intellect and prodigious mental and physical energy.

He believed strongly in fostering academic excellence and excellence in fieldwork by others, and had a high regard for those who shone in these, especially if they did not brag about it. His undergraduate students will remember the quality of his lectures and skilful blackboard drawings. His graduate students, postgraduates and visitors will remember his willing help with arrangements for them to use his Department.

Many who have worked at Culterty, Banchory, and the Department would not have been there if he had not become Regius Professor of Natural History at the University of Aberdeen in 1946. His main great contributions were to the fostering of ecology in Scotland, and to stimulating a rise of behavioural ecology worldwide via opposition to his 1962 book.

VCWE was a complex many-sided character, and a few suffered from his flaws, but far more gained immeasurably from his unstinted capacity to help them and enable scientific work to bloom. In his own unusual way he was an intellectual giant, who carried great stature of personality and authority even simply by his presence. In these days of frequent cheese-paring and bureaucracy in research funding, many must wish he were here again in his vigorous earlier years, as a superb enabler and advocate of excellence in science.

Chapter 5. An unofficial history of the formation of ITE Brathens

(from The Ratcatcher, autumn 1997), the newsletter run by and for those at the former research station of the Institute of Terrestrial Ecology at Hill of Brathens, Banchory

Editorial; comment by editor Dave Carss

Before we start this new series, a word or two about Adam. First, he was recently awarded Honorary Life Membership of WWF-UK 'in recognition of his outstanding quality of work, and a lifetime dedicated to securing the future of the Cairngorms.....we are all optimistic that your work will have ensured better implementation of European conservation legislation in the Cairngorms, and thus made a long-lasting contribution to conservation in the UK's finest mountain landscape.' Not content with securing the future of the Cairngorms, Adam has also written about them. His book *The Cairngorms* was recently voted one of the top 50 'quintessential Scottish books' in a Scotsman/James Thin poll, rubbing shoulders with the likes of Scott, Burns, Neil Gunn, Robert Louis Stevenson and Irvine Welsh. Pretty impressive! So too is this, his latest offering to *Ratcatcher,* .... an unofficial history of events leading to the formation of ITE Brathens (ITE was the Institute of Terrestrial Ecology and a new ITE research station was built at Hill of Brathens near Banchory in the early 1970s)

A serial thriller, Part 1

Henry Ford said history was bunk. He was partly right, for it is a highly subjective indiscipline, prone to fads, fashions, fawnings and political leanings, almost like what is too often over-trumpeted as sound rigorous science! However, knowledge of some past events can help understand the present better. This serial thriller chronicles some factual events that most current occupants of ITE Brathens are unlikely to know. Interpretation of factual events is of course open to various possible different explanations. Doubtless, anyone silly enough to wade through past files of the Nature Conservancy, Aberdeen University and Scottish Landowners' Federation (if relevant files still exist) may write an official history one day. It would be boring, and certainly one-sided and of dubious reliability, because official papers by their nature are so biased and partial.

My history is unofficial, and some information never was in a file. There are hard facts, though my selection and interpretation of them are subjective. I add a few asides that are not central to the story but related to it well enough to help understanding. They bring a touch of humour to leaven some of the officialese, politicking, empire building and other ridiculous aspects of many scientists, lairds, and their organisations and reorganisations.

The initial event was that the Scottish Landowners' Federation, worried by loss of income through lower grouse stocks and bags, decided in 1956 'that a new study of the Red Grouse and moor management would afford valuable and practical results. The Federation requested the Conservancy to carry out the investigation.' *(Report of the Nature Conservancy for the year ended 30th September 1956, p. 25, HMSO, London).*

The NC had been formed in 1949 by a Labour Government aiming to alter society fundamentally, after a war that came close to shattering Britain. The autonomous NC had a small staff with a rapidly increasing commitment to designate reserves and do ecological research on nature conservation in Britain as a whole. The NC's Director General, E.M. Nicholson, had been Secretary to Herbert Morrison, a heavyweight cabinet member of Attlee's post-war socialist government, which made clear it had more important problems to solve than looking after Scottish lairds and their vested interests. The NC's very few research staff in Scotland, such as Jim Lockie and Donald McVean, had to carry out administrative duties and reactions to *ad hoc* lobbying on seals and other matters as well as doing research. The NC could not accede to the SLF request, even though interested in it.

The NC Annual Report continued, 'With their many other commitments the Conservancy were unable to allocate staff or funds for the purpose but the Federation have agreed to finance a pilot enquiry for a period of three years from 1st October, 1956'. Professor V.C. Wynne-Edwards at the University of Aberdeen had heard of the SLF request as he was a Board member of the NC, and he decided to help on his own. He offered to provide the services of his Department of Natural History and the University's administrative section, and to search for suitable scientific staff, while maintaining full liaison with the NC. The Annual Report went on, 'The necessary facilities will therefore be provided and the work carried out under the aegis of the Conservancy by the Natural History Department of Aberdeen University. The Head of the Department, Professor V.C. Wynne-Edwards, who is a member of the Nature Conservancy, will supervise the investigation which will be carried out by a Senior Research Fellow appointed by the University'.

The SLF formed a Grouse Liaison Committee comprised mainly of a wide geographical spread of the more interested Scottish moor owners. On it sat scientific advisor Prof Wynne-Edwards, with the NC also represented by Scottish farmer and ornithologist Arthur B. Duncan (then NC Chairman for Great Britain) and Dr John Berry (NC Director for Scotland). The University would be administrator of SLF funds.

You might wonder what any of this has to do with ITE Brathens. The fact is that if NC had taken up the SLF request for NC to carry out the investigation, the main field work would have been based outside north-east Scotland and nearer to the NC's Scottish office at 12 Hope Terrace in Edinburgh. Probably the main field work would have been on moorland in the Southern Uplands or Stirlingshire. In due course it is likely that the studies on grouse and moorlands would have become an integral part of the research component at NC's Edinburgh office. Subsequently, after ITE's formation, it would have been based at ITE Bush along with the work of other scientific research staff transferred from Hope Terrace. Readers can make up their own minds on whether this would have been better or worse or no different from a Banchory base. That is not part of this serial thriller.

In 1956 the Grouse Liaison Committee had much discussion on the best base for the main field work. Some lairds said it should not be in north-east Scotland near Aberdeen, where grouse generally abounded, but in central, west, or north-west Scotland where the decline was most marked. Wynne-Edwards countered this by saying reasonably big sample sizes would be harder to achieve at low density, and the best progress

would come from study of a high-density area near to the University.

Typically, the lairds forming most of the Committee hadtheir say at meetings but then tended to accept Wynne-Edwards' advice (which in turn would be backed by Arthur Duncan and John Berry). Fortunately they did so on this crucial occasion. Moreover, the Earl of Dalhousie had stolen a lead by offering as the main study area his Invermark moor in Glen Esk, Angus, and also disused shooting lodges as rented accommodation to scientists appointed. As other possibilities were vague, the Earl's offer was accepted.

David Jenkins, a Dennis Chitty student who had done a DPhil study on partridge numbers and behaviour at the Bureau of Animal Population in Oxford, was appointed in late 1956. While assistant lecturer in Wynne-Edwards' department, I had worked for a PhD on ptarmigan populations, including observations on red grouse, and was appointed in late summer 1957. DJ and I were Senior Research Fellows at Aberdeen University.

The Grouse Liaison Committee used to meet mostly at the Station Hotel in Perth, a good central location in Scotland, with DJ and me in attendance to answer questions and take part in detailed discussion. We could tell as soon as we swung through the hotel's main door if the SLF lairds were in, as their voices boomed so loudly. Before we gathered in a private room for the formal meeting, we would all have a drink in the bar followed by lunch in the dining room. Others in bar or dining room would talk quietly, as usual in a big hotel with good soundproofing, making a remarkable contrast with the uninhibited loud voices and laughter of the lairds and their womenfolk turning up after the meeting. They simply took the place over, and shouted as if they were standing in a gale on a windswept hilltop. Aberdeenshire-born author John R. Allan put it well, in his book *North-East Lowlands of Scotland* (1952, Robert Hale, London, p.9), with reference to Deeside, writing "mansions and shooting lodges where parties go out in the morning to shoot birds, accompanied by women whose tweeds are nearly as loud as their voices"!

In 1958 I began exploratory studies of heather ecology in addition to my main work on grouse populations and behaviour. We soon realised that a better understanding of heather ecology in relation to grouse and other moorland animals was of great importance. This led to the appointment of G.R. Miller, who had worked with Charles Gimingham in the Botany Department at Aberdeen, to do more intensive work on heather. Another who was interviewed by Wynne-Edwards, DJ and me was Cedric Milner, who later became senior officer of ITE Bangor. A bright vigorous young scientist, he lacked Gordon's local experience and back-up from Aberdeen's Botany Department. Gordon joined us in Glen Esk, living with wife Lesley in a house beside Dalbrack farm in the upper glen.

The SLF's three-year funding ended on 30 September 1959 as originally agreed, but the understanding from the outset had been that, "if the work then looked promising, the Nature Conservancy would assume financial responsibility for the ensuing stage" (Wynne-Edwards 1960, *6th Progress Report of the Enquiry into the Decline of Red Grouse).* The NC proposed to continue the work by funding it via the University of Aberdeen in the form of a Nature Conservancy Unit of Grouse and Moorland Ecology, with Prof Wynne-Edwards as Honorary Director and Dr C.H. Gimingham of the University's Botany Department as Honorary Botanical Consultant. The Unit was begun as from 1 April 1960, six months after the SLF funding ended and following stopgap NC funding during the six months. The reason for continuing was that the NC had decided that the work had become central to their increasing interest in moorland ecology generally. So, the "Treasury have consented to finance the undertaking, subject to continued progress being made into fundamental problems of moorland ecology" (Wynne-Edwards 1960, above reference). DJ and I became Senior Scientific Officers on NC's staff, and Gordon Miller a Scientific Officer. We lived and worked in Glen Esk until August 1961.

In early 1961 we knew that intensive field work in Glen Esk would end in August, associated with a projected move in August 1961 to a new field base near Banchory in Deeside. There were three reasons for the move. According to local information, the main one was that DJ had antagonised two arrogant powerful gamekeepers by continually arguing with them a', social events (such as Tarfside dances!) that raptor predation on grouse was of little note compared with proper management of the moorland. From an objective viewpoint DJ was right, but the way he said it and the incongruity of the occasions annoyed the keepers. Especially was this so for my next-door neighbour Jock Mitchell, head keeper of Millden, then owned by the Duke of Roxburghe. The Duke, though not on the Liaison Committee, was one of the more powerful Scottish landowners. The complainants made it clear via factor and laird that it would be better if we were "doon the glen". In due course, doon the glen we went, after an interval that allowed other arrangements to be made without disrupting the work too adversely. Some cap-doffing historians might call it a "benign" clearance. However, my daughter young Jenny was a real "glenner", brought up as a glen resident from birth, unlike the absentee lairds and factors with their non-glen accents, language and behaviour.

Of lesser importance was that the Duke used to walk through my garden at Fernybank Lodge next to Millden Lodge on his way to fish his favourite pool on the River North Esk, even though a shorter easier route led through a field, which did not entail opening and closing three sets of gates. On one occasion he was politely requested to consider taking the field route in future, to avoid unnecessarily disturbing the many captive grouse that then occupied pens in the Fernybank front garden. He agreed to do so and showed no annoyance. As he passed the pens on his way to the public road with me after I had made the request, he looked at one unusually vocal and aggressive cock red grouse that threatened us as we came close. The Duke with a loud laugh said "Listen to that silly old bastard, he's telling us how thankful he is to be in your garden and not on the moor on The Twelfth with me in the butts!" All this pointed to his being relaxed, but afterwards we heard Millden underkeeper Jim Campbell that the Duke had been annoyed. This quickly became hot jungle news up and down the glen, with nearly everybody enjoying the story, which rapidly became "Hiv ye heard that Adam Watson threw the Duke o Roxburghe oot o his gairden?" (this would have been an athletic feat beyond me, as the Duke was large, red and rotund). Tossing a small caber would have been easier.

(An aside reveals more about the Duke. Dr John Flux, an Aberdeen University zoology student employed temporarily by DJ to check the age and sex of grouse in the shooting bags, was on the Duke's moor at Millden on one occasion, standing in a butt at the end of a grouse drive while starting to look at shot birds gathered by the keepers at that butt. The Duke, who stood several butts away, shouted to John "How many have you got at your butt?", whereupon John replied "Ten, Sir". The Duke shouted back, loud enough for the entire company of shooters, gamekeepers, beaters, and other helpers to hear, "Not Sir. Your Grace!" Every time I have told this since, the reaction from folk is to laugh but doubt the story's truth, as surely nobody could be that arrogant, pompous and stupid? But true it was. Also, the trailer cart that carried lunch hampers up the hill and baskets of dead grouse down the hill, had "His Grace the Duke of Roxburghe" in conspicuous gold lettering on its side. Such events tell much about the wisdom and humility of our hereditary peerage.

The third reason for our having to leave Glen Esk as the main base was that the SLF did not wish to continue funding beyond the agreed three years. Moreover, the study had led to our emphasising that moor management was the key to the grouse decline and how to reverse it. Most lairds on the Committee, and other lairds not on it, did not like being told their own management was the main problem. They preferred scapegoat issues outwith their control, such as raptor predation, disease, hikers, sheep, lack of sheep, etc etc. There had been about as many ideas for the cause of the grouse decline as there were lairds round the Committee table. Only this lack of agreement among them, together with their tendency to accept Wynne-Edwards' solemn pronouncements that the scientific workers had to be given their heads, prevented us from being ordered to do work that would have been virtually worthless in scientific terms as well as a waste of the lairds' money.

When the Earl decided to end the main Glen Esk work, he agreed that I could return to the part that I had studied most intensively, for observations from a land rover on territorial behaviour, numbers, and survival for as many years as I wished, but no other work was to be done, and no others were to be allowed except in the land rover with me.

Wynne-Edwards saw the enforced move as an opportunity. We had described events at Glen Esk, but could not do experiments, other than ending shooting on a small area for a few years, and taking some eggs for hatching in captivity. Wynne-Edwards thought we

should move nearer the University and find a new area in lower Deeside where we could rent the shooting and manage the land, and so be able to do experiments central to the study. He was later proved right, as the move did lead to many experiments to test hypotheses, and so advanced reliable understanding more rapidly.

We inspected various moors, decided that Kerloch near Banchory was the best, and Wynne-Edwards clinched a rental deal with owner Sir William Gladstone. The next step was to look for a possible office. The best place was Blackhall Stables two miles from Banchory on the south side of Dee. Although disused since wartime occupation by the Indian army and mules, it was in good condition and merely required renovation, decoration, and installing electricity, telephone and other services.

Assistant Dudley Pinnock joined us in the last Glen Esk year, and all of us worked from our new rented homes in the Banchory area until Blackhall was ready in January 1963. My wife Jenny was appointed secretary for the first half of each day, typing and looking after four staff and a Canadian student as well as running the office for the University and the NC, and making the all-important tea. It was quite a change from her job before we went to Glen Esk, as Secretary to the hugely ambitious D.J. Finney FRS, with his big Department of Statistics and Agricultural Research Council's Statistics Unit at Aberdeen University. Young Jenny, not yet at Drumoak school, was a seventh Blackball occupant.

Robert Moss, whom I met at the Edward Grey Institute's Annual New Year Conference at Oxford in 1963, was interested when I mentioned evidence I had found that grouse eggs varied inherently in quality and that spring density and breeding success of red grouse and ptarmigan (and the density of mountain hares) were related to the base-richness of underlying bedrock and soils. He suggested contributing his biochemical knowledge to help get a better understanding of the mechanisms involved in such ecological problems, and I thought this a good idea. Robert came up to see us at Blackhall in February 1963, and wasn't put off when I took him past snow-blocked public roads on to the moor at Corndavon, where virtually all the base-rich vegetation I had mentioned was totally buried under a deep compact blanket of snow. Following two Canadian post-graduate students Don Eastman and

Harold Cumming, he became our first post-graduate PhD student on a problem about red grouse, in his case emphasising nutrition and the highly selective chemical composition of food eaten versus food available. Robert became a member of the Unit staff in 1966, and you can read more about it in Part II of this serial thriller.

Nick Picozzi was appointed an assistant in 1963. He and Roy Dennis were on the short leet and I was interviewing with V.C Wynne-Edwards. When VCWE asked Roy Dennis why he had applied to be assistant in the grouse unit, Roy replied "I want to become Director General of the Nature Conservancy". VCWE and I did not reply, but I could see VCWE's stern face, before he changed tack by asking a question on a totally different topic. His response to me after RD left the room was short. That was RD right out, and so NP in! During 1964, Raymond Parr was appointed as a new assistant. Others, including Mick Marquiss and Raymond Hewson, came later. Read all about it in Part II!

Banchory soon became a name well known to many scientists from numerous countries who came to visit us and see the work. We even had a Finn, Dr Matti Helminen, saying that after reading our scientific papers he had for years wanted to come to Banchory. He delivered this with near-reverence as he saw the village sign, saying "At last I am at Banchory!", almost like a pilgrim to Mecca! I had difficulty in suppressing a laugh, but managed to smile. Matti was totally serious, like many Finns. So ends Part I of the unofficial history, with Blackhall by Banchory as the centre of operations, only a few miles by road (and 1.5 miles as the crow flies) from the current ITE Hill of Brathens.

A serial thriller, Part 2

Part 1 ended with the establishment of an office and research base at Blackhall near Banchory in 1963. Part 2 describes some of the events until the late 1960s, when some of the Nature Conservancy's research staff from Edinburgh and Merlewood were sent to Blackhall in anticipation of a new Banchory research station being built in later years. Like Part 1 it is selective, but does chronicle some of the main factual events. It describes also some revealing incidents that help elucidate understanding of the empire-building and other behavioural aspects of a few of the main movers, and adds a few amusing asides to leaven the fare.

The grouse research at Kerloch moor depended on renting the shooting lease from landowner Sir William Gladstone of Fasque, but the moor was also rented from him for hill grazing of sheep and cattle by tenant farmers Mr Minty of Pitreadie and Mr Petrie of Midtown. We needed to get on well with the farmers, as we had to work on their hill grazings with dogs that were often near their sheep and cattle. To aid this, David Jenkins gave each of them a bottle of whisky every Christmas, paid out of the Unit's petty cash. As the University finance staff might have queried this, DJ decided that each receipt from the local shop should state "To one roll of barbed wire". The finance staff never asked why so many rolls of wire were being bought. The naming of the goods as "barbed" wire might seem ironic, given the stinging effect of a big dram of whisky down someone's throat, but I think irony was not intended. When subsequently appointed officer-in-charge in 1966, I terminated the practice. In any case I thought there were better ways to improve relations, such as speaking in the north-east dialect of the Scots language with the farmers and their families, and the annual Crathes party for them and others (below).

In the mid 1960s, Paul Bramley came as a PhD student on marked roe deer at a study area at Cheddington wood in Dorset, supervised by DJ. The latter was now doing increasingly less fieldwork and more administration by his choice, and started looking for promotion and a new job supervising more staff. Years before in 1957, when he came north to Aberdeen University as a Senior Research Fellow and someone asked about his ambition in life, he replied, "To sit at a big desk and be in charge of many people"! Perhaps you might disapprove of this, but at least he called a spade a spade.

In 1966 the Nature Conservancy decided to have a new post of Assistant Director (Research) in Scotland to run its rapidly expanding research staff. This was to be in complement with a new Assistant Director (Conservation) in Scotland, which was to go to former North-west Highlands Regional Officer Dr John Morton Boyd. The job of Assistant Director (Research) was just what DJ had in mind.

Some able candidates brought stiff competition, but DJ had a flying start for interview. Knowing that no-holds-barred discussion and criticism at the

Blackhall tea-room table and blackboards often led to clearer thinking and new ideas, he gave an internal Blackhall seminar with his outline of the NC's ideal future research in Scotland, and from the rest of us sought criticism, both destructive and constructive. He got both in good measure, mainly from Gordon Miller and me. Outlines on the blackboard were rubbed out and new ones inserted by us and him, until he eventually had the mutually agreed best outline, with accompanying rationale, justification, and literature references. Mrs Elspet Weir, appointed in late 1963 as first full-time typist, wrote down the blackboard contents in shorthand and typed this for further editing by Gordon, DJ and me. No other interview candidate had done such impressive homework. DJ was in with a shout!

The NC then appointed me as officer-in-charge at the Blackhall base of the NC's Unit of Grouse and Moorland Ecology, which was still attached to Aberdeen University with Prof. V.C. Wynne-Edwards as Honorary Director. New staff members were appointed at the NC's Edinburgh base to do research on red deer, vegetation, freshwater ecology, and vertebrate predators. DJ was finding it difficult to run the red deer study on Rum, as he and the team had become bogged down for a variety of personal and other reasons. He asked me to take charge of it under his overall supervision, but I did not fancy being bogged down too, so politely declined his offer.

At the NC's main Scottish office in Edinburgh, DJ still hankered after Deeside, and wished to transfer most of his Edinburgh-based research staff to Banchory. His flair for continual lobbying came fully into play. The eventual outcome was that he managed to persuade the NC in 1967 to decide to build a new research station at Banchory, and "in anticipation, several additional members of staff were posted to Blackhall" (*The Nature Conservancy Research in Scotland, Report for 1968–70*, 1970, p. 1). These early moves during 1967 involved John Miles and Wilson J. Kinnaird being transferred from Edinburgh to Blackhall, and David Welch (who had studied sheep grazing and vegetation at Moorhouse National Nature Reserve in northern England) from Merlewood to Blackhall.

A new four-roomed hut was erected in 1967 outside the Blackhall back-door, to house John, Wilson, and David. Into the fourth room moved Gordon Miller, who had left his larger downstairs office in the main building to afford more space for the rapidly expanding library that was in the same room and to get more privacy from the many new library-users. Roger Cummins and Ian Paterson were appointed to the botanical team in 1969, Ann Veitch as an assistant (later to marry John Miles), and other assistants such as Eddie Kemp and Mike Dyer, of whom the last-named later flowered greatly in non-biological academia. Subsequently the new hut was shifted to Brathens, and now stands separate beyond the west end of the main building, next to the fields.

In the mid 1960s the Glen Feshie Estate, long owned along with Glen Tromie and Gaick by the Macpherson-Grant family of Ballindalloch, was advertised for sale. The NC wanted to buy it, at the then going rate of £85 000 (now £6 million, following major capital gains by three owners). Much of the estate formed a valuable section of the Cairngorms National Nature Reserve, including some remnants of old native pinewood and birchwood, great tracts of outstanding alpine ground, and an unusual braided river. Moreover, the NC thought it important to extend the deer research to a mainland deer-forest, as there had been criticism that the study on the Isle of Rum was atypical because the sea constrained deer movements.

Mr George Pottinger, a top mandarin civil servant at the Scottish Office, blocked the NC's attempt to buy Glen Feshie Estate. He was alleged by senior NC staff to have said "The Nature Conservancy already has too much power in the Cairngorms". Lord Dulverton, one of the cigarette-manufacturing Wills family, then bought the estate. Only years later did the police arrest Mr George Pottinger. After being taken to court, he entered jail at Her Majesty's pleasure for a long number of years, on corruption charges. He had been involved with Yorkshire architect John Poulsen in shady deals involving large sums of public money. The associated Speyside connection was that both men were involved in unbridled major hotel and other tourist developments at Aviemore close to Glen Feshie! Local NC staff in Speyside reckoned that Mr Pottinger wanted the unbridled growth of tourism developments in the Aviemore area and nearby to continue for reasons of obvious Pottinger/Poulsen axes to grind. A more confident and powerful NC that owned far more land in the area might threaten or curb this.

Despite its failure to buy the estate, the NC still

wished to do deer research in Glen Feshie. I recollect attending a meeting of about 20 vertebrate ecologists, mostly from NC staff but including Frank Fraser Darling, and US range ecologist Thane Riney who had worked in Africa for the UN Food and Agriculture Organisation. DJ had organised the meeting and we spent a day in the glen, evaluating the pros and cons of working there. Lord Dulverton had already removed all the sheep, and had firmly decided to form large deer-fenced coniferous plantations with the deer excluded, and to fertilize alluvial grasslands for deer foraging. Clearly, big changes in land use and management were already in place or had been firmly decided for implementation in the near future. The foregone conclusion stared out that the place was a dog's breakfast as a site for large-scale scientific study of habitat, as it formed an experiment with no pre-experiment baseline and no control. Everyone present said the NC should go elsewhere for the research, with the exception of Ian A. Nicholson who was to be in charge of the new work, DJ who had brought us together for consultation, and Director of Research Dr Martin J. Holdgate who was based at the NC's London HQ at Belgrave Square. They listened to the rest of us but gave no opinion. The rest of us went away, thinking the consultation meeting had been conclusive and hence worthwhile, for all its high costs in money and time.

Despite the unequivocally clear results of this consultation, powerful imperial motivation held sway later, and a large new 'Range Ecology Team' of deer biologists and botanists was formed to use Glen Feshie as the main study area. The NC's Director (Scotland) Dr W. Joe Eggeling and the NC's Director of Research (UK) Dr Martin J. Holdgate agreed with DJ and Ian Nicholson. I recollect that not one of the working research scientists directed to the project believed the area to be good for the proposed study. They complained to us and others, but not with a single united loud voice to the 'high heid yins' or the public, so the high heid yins got their way.

Although some useful studies were done there later and published, the scheme as a whole proved pretty much a fiasco and a waste of public money. As Neil Bayfield aptly put it when giving a farewell speech at Brathens on 31 October 1997 on the occasion of Ian Paterson's last day on ITE staff, "a great amount of energy was expended and work done, but in the end not very much came out of it"! In addition, this period blighted the careers of several of the scientists, although not because of the Feshie scheme alone, as the behaviour of those in charge played a role.

It should be noted also that not all the failures were those of the NC's top staff who took the main decisions and ran the team. At the outset, Lord Dulverton had given his word that he would reduce hind numbers in one part of the glen, as part of the agreed research and management scheme. Later he decided not to implement this. When DJ remonstrated, Lord Dulverton threatened, saying "David, if you continue this I'll take you and the Nature Conservancy all the way to the House of Lords". This was David and Goliath again, except that this time Goliath had all the big rocks to throw!

An aside on this is revealing. When the independent-minded forthright E. Max Nicholson retired as the NC's Director-General (UK), the government removed the NC's independence as an autonomous body, because the NC had stepped on the toes of vested land interests and bigger government departments that wished old ways to continue. In the NC's early days of 1952, the Board of 18 included 12 scientists with men of the calibre of Charles Elton, E.B. Ford, Professor W.H. Pearsall, and Chairman Professor A.G. Tansley, and two prominent amateur ornithologists. To have such un-decent chaps in charge was a most un-British way of running a government body, especially when powerful vested private and state land interests sometimes were being asked to change their ways ever so slightly! In subsequent decades under governments both Labour and Conservative, the proportion of scientists became drastically lower and that of vested land interests correspondingly higher.

The new Director-General appointed to the emasculated NC was kilt-wearing Scottish botanist Dr Duncan Poore, who agreed to the Glen Feshie research scheme. Oily, smooth, unctuous, woolly and weak, he would have been a little-finger pushover for Lord Dulverton, whose very face and look signified total dominance without the need to say anything. Dr Poore did not forbid Dulverton's flagrant breaching of the key founding principle of the Cairngorms National Nature Reserve, which that there should be natural evolution of habitats with a minimum of human interference. In particular, the

NC under Dr Poore allowed Lord Dulverton to bulldoze 13 km of vehicle tracks within the NNR, to plant coniferous trees densely, including North American species planted under ancient Caledonian Scots pines, to plough hillsides for planting, and to erect miles of deer fencing.

In 1996 Dr Poore, now Professor and retired, popped up again at a meeting in a hall at Kincraig in Badenoch, this time as scientific adviser to "conservation" trust Will Woodlands. Despite his stated adviser status, he had the effrontery to chair the meeting on behalf of Will Woodlands. No less oily than I had remembered, he well exemplified the proverb that the leopard does not change its spots. Will Woodlands had bought Glen Feshie from Englishman John Dibben, who had made his pile from a kitchen-furniture company registered in the tax-avoidance haven of the Windward Islands. The trust wished to erect new fenced exclosures for natural regeneration of native trees and yet another for planting, and refused to reduce deer numbers quickly to allow natural tree regeneration. At the Kincraig meeting in late 1996, Professor Poore backed the Will Woodlands scheme to the hilt as a conservation project, despite the scheme's obvious flaws. He did so in the face of concerted opposition from Scottish voluntary conservation, mountaineering and recreational bodies who had come to the meeting. Mark Gibson, a member of staff on Brodies the Edinburgh land agents, who was their main adviser to Will Woodlands, later referred in a letter in the press to Professor Poore's "impeccable conservation credentials"! It was *deja vu* again, with Poore continuing to support damaging schemes in Glen Feshie, just as he had supinely done in the 1960s.

Meanwhile in 1972 the NC had been split into the Nature Conservancy Council and the Institute of Terrestrial Ecology. Dr Poore departed for the greener pastures of an Oxford Professorship of Forestry and the International Union for the Conservation of Nature (where he blocked and pigeon-holed Professor Kai Curry-Lindahl's highly critical 1974 report on the poor state of conservation in the Cairngorms and the NC's undue deference to private landowners there). Martin Holdgate left the old NC, in meteoric flight for high promotion. John Jeffers became Director of ITE. JJ had long thought little of the range ecology team (now lower case) and its Glen Feshie work, and

soon the team was broken up, a sound decision that should have been taken years earlier.

Glen Feshie was now left to the domineering Lord Dulverton. Thenceforth he could bully only NCC staff locally and nationally, and threaten with legal action (in tandem with neighbour Lt Col. J.P. "Ian" Grant of Rothiemurchus) me for publishing critical comment on the state of nature conservation in the Cairngorms area. Such was their influence that for some years Ian Grant was on NC's main Board, and later Lord Dulverton on NCC's Scottish Committee. Lord Dulverton even sat on the Red Deer Commission's Board as NERC's scientific representative, next to a run of years when NERC's representative was none other than the Duke of Atholl, a couple of facts once told to us at Brathens somewhat shamefacedly by NERC's then Secretary R.J.H. Beverton. So much for the independence of public scientific bodies as applied to UK issues where vested land interests hold sway!

In the mid 1960s, severe vegetation damage and soil erosion had occurred as a result of unchecked use of tracked machines in the new ski developments at Cairn Gorm, and the NC asked me to form and lead a small team on human impact in mountain areas. I said yes. Indeed, it was largely my preliminary observation of the seriousness of the problems that led to NC's recognition that research was required. Neil Bayfield was appointed in late 1967 to join this team at Blackhall, and soon afterwards an assistant Stanley Moyes who now lives at Finzean and is in charge of the Bucket Mill there.

As the work of the Grouse Unit had widened more and more into moorland ecology generally, the NC decided in 1968 to wind it up as a University Unit and incorporate the entire Unit staff into the staff complement of the NC itself. In 1968, Blackhall became the NC's Mountain and Moorland Research Station. Appointed officer-in-charge, I continued in this role until the Hill of Brathens station was built and occupied in November 1972.

After DJ went to Edinburgh, he soon favoured ending the grouse work. He said all the most important conclusions had been reached already during the years when he was on the grouse team, and only some minor details remained to be discovered. The cake was complete, and although a little icing was possible, it was an unnecessary luxury! As Assistant Director

(Research) for all the NC's large research staff in Scotland, he had much influence. DJ had unending energy for lobbying, and lobbied senior and junior staff vigorously and frequently. Soon, he started to bring pressure about this on me.

I remember a meeting with him over coffee in the palatial red lounge of the Raemoir Hotel, with the NC's outstanding field botanist and ornithologist Dr Derek A. Ratcliffe present. The meeting, which had been completely amicable among three close colleagues, suddenly became frosty when DJ abruptly announced that he intended to end the grouse work and shift the grouse team on to other topics. Already I had had tempting offers of good research jobs in North America, which included bringing Robert Moss and others with me if they and I so wished. I told DJ that if he insisted on implementing his intention, I would leave and head "up the road" without hesitation. He replied menacingly, "I may call your bluff on that". The meeting then ended when I left. In the event later, he dropped his plan totally. For once, discretion was the better part of valour, for although he did not know about the North American offers and I did not tell him, my determination worried him. At the Raemoir meeting, Derek Ratcliffe, who was a senior scientist on NC staff in England and had no locus whatever in the political matter being discussed, had sat silent and utterly astonished as DJ raised this private matter in open confrontation, with DR present.

Later that day I told the Grouse Unit's Honorary Director Prof V.C. Wynne-Edwards what was happening. Having listened, he thought DJ would back down, and so saw no need to intervene. Nevertheless, he advised me to apply for a DSc degree at Aberdeen University, using my collected papers on population regulation and behaviour in northern birds and mammals, as this would strengthen my hand in any similar incidents that might arise again in future. I had never considered doing something like this for political reasons, but took his advice, applied, and in due course received the degree. In retrospect, however, I think his support stiffened my determination and confidence more than any university degree.

In a subsequent year after the University Unit had been wound up, DJ again raised the proposal to close the grouse work and shift us to other topics, and this time strengthened his position beforehand by managing to persuade Dr Martin Holdgate, who was then still the NC's Director of Research (Britain), to consider it seriously. After DJ put his proposal to me, with a strong hint that MH agreed, I went to Aberdeen to see Prof V.C. Wynne-Edwards. VCWE said that if they implemented the threat, he would be prepared, if I agreed, to form a new research group at Aberdeen University to continue the work under University funding, supporting me, Robert Moss, and any others whom I wished. Quickly he made private soundings in the University to ensure that the scheme could be put in place at short notice if and when needed. The answer was a clear Yes.

When I told DJ this, he was flabbergasted. It took the wind right out of his sails, and he sulked. Shortly after, I recall a train journey when Martin Holdgate, DJ and I went south from Aberdeen. When DJ was temporarily in the toilet, MH raised the subject of DJ's wish to end the NC grouse work, told me it would not happen, and asked me to send him a typed account of what I wanted for the future grouse work in terms of staff and money. He said obviously he could not guarantee he could give all I might ask, but he would do his best and see that there would be a workable team with good back-up. I said I would let him have the typed account. It was all over in one minute flat! A man with a flair for summing up complex meetings, seeing a solution to total deadlock at meetings, and getting everybody to agree with his summary and solution, he managed to solve this particular problem with grace, good humour, and continuing good relations with Robert, DJ, and me. Ironically, this episode strengthened our hand more than anything we might have initiated spontaneously ourselves.

The final compromise resulted in Gordon Miller and Nick Picozzi being off the grouse team, although both continued to work at Blackhall. Gordon became part of Ian Nicholson's large Range Ecology Team. So did Neil Bayfield, although he wisely managed to keep his own little kingdom of human impact partly intact rather than being an integral central part of the Nicholsonian empire. This was neatly arranged with me still providing some advice on human impact to Neil, from outside the Range Ecology Team, as I was still doing research on human impact myself. Nick studied crows and raptors, with DJ supervising.

Part 2 ended in 1969 after the formation of the Nature Conservancy's Mountain and Moorland Research Station at Blackhall and a rapid big expansion of staff based there, in anticipation of a new Banchory research station. In the event, the NC did not have the funds immediately available to build the new station until 1970. Still based at Edinburgh as Assistant Director for Research (Scotland), David Jenkins was beginning to expand the NC's research on vertebrate predators.

Supervised by DJ, Nick Picozzi was studying crows at Kerloch near Banchory, and later common buzzards in Speyside, and then hen harriers in Glen Dye and eventually Orkney. DJ formed a Predator Research Group comprising Dr Ian Newton who was now on NC staff studying sparrowhawks in Dumfries-shire, Nick Picozzi and associated outside people such as the RSPB's Hon. Douglas N. Weir on Speyside, who worked with Nick on buzzards, and myself because of my studies of golden eagles and ptarmigan preda-tion. The report *The Nature Conservancy Research in Scotland* (1970, p. 2) states 'The Predator Research group was started in 1969, as a development of the Assistant Director's Laboratory'. The report *Institute of Terrestrial Ecology Research in Scotland , Report for 1971*–73, p. 2) noted that 'The newest recruit to this research group is Dr Harris whose very wide previous experience of sea-birds has brought him actively in contact with workers in this field throughout Britain and also in many other parts of the world'.

In reality, the NC Predator Research Group was little more than a window-dressing cosmetic paper group of disparate individuals who happened for one reason or another to be doing some study of vertebrate predators. It certainly did not function as a coherent group that co-ordinated its activities with full co-oper-ation for the mutual enhanced benefit of both the group and the individuals who comprised it.

On one occasion, DJ, Ian Newton and I were in Ian's car at Edinburgh, where there was a meeting at NC's Scottish HQ at Hope Terrace. Ian, just appointed, had arrived to meet other NC staff and become familiar with the organisation. When we were all seated in the car, DJ directed a remarkable piece of overt aggres-sive dominance behaviour towards Ian. It reminded me of Schjelderup-Ebbe's classical peck-order studies of poultry, where the top cock is overwehelmingly

domineering within seconds of an outsider young cockerel being introduced. In later years, Ian and DJ developed a more reasonable *modus operandi*, and Ian went on to become an eminent scientist better known than DJ, but I have little doubt that the incident in the car will be remembered even more clearly by Ian than by me! After other unusual incidents involving people other than Ian, the NC Director (Scotland) Dr J. Morton Boyd put DJ on probation for a year.

During the late 1960s, Mick Marquiss did his PhD work at Blackhall on the behaviour of captive red grouse, with Robert Moss as his main supervisor. Brian Staines, who had been working for a number of years in a London bank, decided he wanted a complete change, and applied to do a PhD studying red deer. While down in London for a committee meeting, Prof V.C.Wynne-Edwards interviewed Brian at Heathrow Airport and decided to offer him a student-ship. Aberdeen University then became deer-shooting tenant of Glen Dye estate, and Brian did his study with Prof Wynne-Edwards representing the University as nominal tenant, me as the main PhD supervisor, and Brian co-ordinating closely with head-keeper Dan Dowell. Such a tenuous complex arrangement on a private estate would normally be difficult to imple-ment successfully, but because Brian and I both got on very well with Dan, it worked.

One of the reasons for our good relations with the Deeside keepers was that by now we were organising an annual party at Crathes Hall for those keepers on land where we had study areas. From Kerloch near Banchory up to Luibeg in the Cairngorms they came for the evening at Crathes. One or two Grouse Team members privately paid for the Hall, much of the food, and the beer, soft drinks, whisky, tea and coffee. Several wives of staff members brought food. To the party each year came the Kerloch tenant farmers, as did every-body from Blackhall including the cleaners, a few from Culterty such as Harry Milne and Ian Patterson, and other visitors such as Desmond Nethersole-Thompson, raptor enthusiasts "Skitts" Rae and Jonathan Hardey, and a few Etchachan Club climbers such as Norman Keir, Raymond Simpson and Stewart Murray. Most brought their spouses or partners.

We provided entertainment in the form of opera from Brian Staines, comedy by Robert Moss and others, songs by me, and at one of the best parties a remarkable demonstration of magical tricks by an Aberdonian friend of mine Ronnie Winram, who cut a lady in half and performed other amazing feats in bright electric light to a largely scientific audience who had not a clue how he managed to do it. Glen Muick head-keeper Dan Fraser played the fiddle very well, and another keeper played an accordion. Balmoral keeper Charlie Wright played the bagpipes, even though chary of doing so in the company of invited guest Miss Bessie Brown of Banchory in her wheel-chair, well-known formidable veteran piping expert and judge. Ray Parr and his country/western band and its electric amplifiers outdid even Charlie for decibels, raising Ray's singing to the rooftops. There was also Scottish and other dancing for the many who wanted to take part.

For food we had greylag and pink-footed geese, mountain hares, rabbits, red grouse, ptarmigan, capercaillie, black grouse, partridge, pheasant, venison of red and roe deer, and salmon, in large quantities cooked by Gray the local baker in Banchory, as well as sausages, bradies and haggis. There were also dozens of hard-boiled bantam eggs, sometimes painted in exotic red colours. Before one of the parties, we labelled the various dishes with the Latin names of the species. The keepers and farmers thought the free party one of the best nights of the year, and there is no doubt it greatly strengthened relations between them and the researchers. Despite the unlimited free booze, none of the visitors or residents ever became tipsy or aggressive.

Ray Hewson, an exciseman at whisky distilleries in Banffshire, had done much study on marked mountain hares. A prominent member of the Mammal Society who had written many papers on a wide variety of topics, Ray was already well known to us at Blackhall and Culterty. The Vertebrate Ecology Group, a small informal group of the most active vertebrate ecologists in Scotland, who met once a year for a weekend to view a field study in depth, once stayed at Keith in Banffshire to inspect the Hewson work, during the late 1960s. On a frosty night in November we walked through snow on his study area at Jock's Hill near Dufftown, to mark and release hares caught in his stopped snares.

As we came off the hill down to the highest hill farm, the farmer appeared immediately and expectantly, almost as if he had been watching our every move and knew exactly when to pounce. We soon saw why (next paragraph). First, however, I must explain that many distilleries give a large daily amount of whisky free to every worker, as a means of preventing theft. More importantly, whisky evaporates, and the Inland Revenue has long set a reasonable allowance for such evaporation, when calculating the amount of tax due from the distillery. If the amount of whisky left exceeds the evaporation allowance, you can see the possibilities if the resident exciseman, distillery manager, stillman and other relevant crucial individuals all agree on what is allowable, strictly within legal limits of course.

When the Vertebrate Ecology Group gathered at the farm, Ray took horn cups out of his car and produced a bottle of over-proof whisky. The first cupful went to the farmer, who downed it in well-practised form and was then given another (Ray often used the farm barn as a forward field base and occasionally for a ceilidh). Soon the rest of us enjoyed sipping a superb dram, and note the word "sipping". Sabbatical post-doctoral visitor Dr Fred Zwickel from the USA got his horn cup like everybody else, but assumed that the whisky was at the usual strength of 70-80% proof. He downed it in a single quick gulp, and then coughed and spluttered, unable to speak, struggling for breath, and not fully recovering until after ten minutes had passed in my vehicle as I drove to Keith. After all, Ray's liquor was strong enough to act as a preservative to the lining of Fred's throat!

Although Ray enjoyed his distillery work and it gave him many opportunities during the day for study of natural history, he yearned to spend more time on research, and decided like Brian Staines that he wanted a complete change. I remember meeting him for tea in a Dufftown cafe, hearing his suggestions, and then deciding I would back a proposal to have him on the staff of the grouse team, working with Robert Moss on the captive birds. This was later agreed by those in charge of the NC, and Ray was duly appointed. At Blackhall there were other students and staff besides those I have mentioned so far, but I do not write further about them here, as they did not include anyone who has been based at Brathens in recent years.

An unusual visitor was the sister of infamous Patty Hearst, daughter of US multi-millionaire Randolph Hearst. Patty Hearst had gone to the opposite extreme from her father, by joining a small but widely known left-wing international group that practised violent action. Professor A. Starker Leopold of Berkeley

University, son of Professor Aldo Leopold of literary and ecological fame, had long been in contact with us over ecological research, had been to visit us at Blackhall, had stayed in my house, and had me staying in his house when I visited Berkeley in 1968. Starker approached me with a view to having Patty's ecologist sister work at Blackhall, out of the intense media limelight that faced the Hearsts in California. I was sympathetic to international cooperation, and one or two people at the top of our organisation agreed to the proposal. Apart from them, the local Banchory police, and my closest research colleague at Blackhall, no one else knew the background. She came to stay with her journalist husband for some months, but never seemed really happy or enthusiastic. The visit was ended prematurely when her father and mother flew across the Atlantic to see her. Unwisely they did not take precautions to travel as incognito as possible, and had RANDOLPH HEARST in large lettering on their luggage. Once the press knew from this lapse what was going on, the idea of the quiet stay at Blackhall out of the media spotlight vanished. She had to return home with her parents to try the near-impossible, how to live a normal media-free life, given such a father and such a sister. I never heard from her again. I cannot now recall her first name, so little did she register as a personality.

Meanwhile the scientists posted from Edinburgh and Merlewood were increasing the number of people at Blackhall, in addition to new staff directly appointed to work at Blackhall such as Neil Bayfield, plus extra new assistants for the scientists. At one stage at Blackhall I was officer in charge of up to 24 people including two full-time typists Mrs Weir and Mrs Edmond, and on average had to spend a third of my time on administration. I was lucky to be able to reduce administration time to one third, but it was mainly a result of the efficiency that results from a small group (see R. Moss's letter to *Nature* on this explosive topic) and on the fact that we were in the backwoods a long way from London and even Edinburgh. Pinstripe-suited sooth-moother gents at high administrative level seldom ventured this far into the wild northlands, other than rare fleeting visits on hot sunny days in summer, when they would make ridiculous remarks such as "You chaps are really lucky to be working here in pleasant countryside in such fine weather, when we have to sweat it out with hard work in city offices". They looked like ducks out of water.

In those days it was standing room only in the tea room during periods when everybody was at the building, almost like a very crowded cocktail party with inadequate room for circulating. The ideal of having in the tea room a single coherent group conversation on scientific matters, which often happened in previous years and in later ones, was impossible in those days, except when most of the inhabitants were away in the field during the summer, at the Glen Feshie project and elsewhere.

The increases of scientific staff, secretarial staff and students at Blackhall required extra rooms to be renovated and other new facilities such as laboratories. Len Taylor, then a Banchory joiner, would usually put in the lowest tender and get the work, irrespective of whether it was joinery, electrical, plumbing or other. As the electrical installations were added piecemeal, the system as a whole became more and more complicated. The fuse-boxes and associated wiring looked superficially like a maze. Anyhow, the electricity supply would frequently fail and we would be plunged suddenly into darkness. The usual cry would go up "Blast, that's Len Taylor again"! On a few days when the power went off in Banchory too, it was claimed by some that this was a knock-on Blackhall Taylor-effect. It was even alleged once that the Banchory fish-and-chipper in the street behind the Burnett Arms was out of action and had no chips for sale because of the Blackhall effect, but I think that was maybe taking credulity too far.

Len was also an undertaker, and had a thin body and heavily-lined bony face topped by a shock of long grey hair. He spoke with a shaking jaw and quavering voice. When he had something to tell us, he would often prefix it with a solemn whisper "atween these four waas (walls) only". He used to state gravely of how ghostly and mysterious Blackhall became at night, especially in the courtyard with its many shadows in the moonlight. On one occasion he was walking quietly into the courtyard, after unlocking the massive tall double gate, when he heard a creaking sound like a door opening behind him. Turning in fright and expecting to see something awful, he realised with fervent relief that it was our extremely tame old cock ptarmigan, which occupied a cage projecting furthest into the courtyard, and challenged anybody coming near that cage with a mechanical-like hoarse snoring croak.

On another occasion at Blackhall at night, Len nearly killed himself. While checking the electrical wiring above the ceilings at night, feeling his way slowly in the darkness, he suddenly received a big electrical shock. He got much more than a shock, but also a bad fright, as his mind again dwelt on the possible supernatural eeriness of Blackhall. Instead of "the deil's awa wi the exciseman", it was maybe "the deil's awa wi the undertaker". Shaking to the core, he turned his torch on the spot where he had felt the shock, and was relieved to see he had merely touched bare copper wires, the rubber insulation having been eaten off by rats! There wis nae Blackhall deil efter aa!

Len once got the job of installing an extra toilet near the back door, and we had to use a temporary portable toilet outside for a day or two while the indoor work was done. Meanwhile for the convenience of all he placed a small portable wooden hut over the outside toilet, somewhat like a wooden sentry box except that it had a door that could be closed and locked from inside. He did not weigh it down, knowing that Blackhall was a very sheltered spot, surrounded by magnificent tall specimen conifer trees. Unfortunately, a wind did rise suddenly on the second day and blew the wooden toilet box on to the top of Paul Bramley's car. Paul could ill afford the cost of the garage repairs and paintwork, and put in a claim to Len Taylor. The latter calmly announced that he could not be held responsible, as it was an act of God! Our response was that God may work "in mysterious ways", and it is well recognised that this includes floods, volcanoes, typhoons, and other natural catastrophes, but it was surely a novel experience for Him to throw a toilet on to a car roof!

Eventually, DJ's plan was to move Ian Nicholson, Brian Mitchell, and Dan McGowan too, and himself, to a new research station at Banchory, which would also house the extra staff sent earlier up to Blackhall. As officer-in-charge of the NC's Banchory station at Blackhall, I was asked by the NC's Edinburgh-based Land Agent John Arbuthnott (now Viscount Arbuthnott, Lord Lieutenant of Kincardineshire), to inspect and evaluate possible sites. As Len Taylor was like a walking encyclopaedia on anything to do with Banchory, its people and surroundings (he still has a remarkable knowledge of this), I enlisted his help. We explored about half a dozen sites, and I wrote a report with Len's help, describing ownership, facilities, and pros and cons. One of the most likely possibilities was the flat freely drained site of the railway station and adjacent extensive yards, later used for a large amount of housing and the Fire Station.

DJ did not like any of the sites, as he was keen on a small estate in the country. In any case, it turned out that none could be bought. The NC as a public body had to abide by the District Valuer's price, and in every case this was exceeded for both seller and buyer, as development pressures were beginning to rise in the Banchory area. Eyes then fell upon Hill of Brathens and its adjoining woodland. Here the DV's price was low, as an earlier application for planning approval of bungalows had been refused and the site was short of water. The NC was therefore able to buy the site at the DV's price.

At the end of a narrow road on the line of the present road, a small house stood between the present west hut and the present library, and the long green shed (now beside the workshop) still stands where it originally did. The last part of the road to the house was later covered with subsoil and topsoil, and occupied an area now forming part of the lawn. An ex tea-planter had built the house, and lived in the long green shed beside the present car park while the house was under construction. One end of the shed housed a store, and the other end (where the wind tunnel is now) was a chicken house. He erected several outbuildings and fenced enclosures, and kept foxes in an enclosure beside the wooden hut that still stands uphill from the north end of the four-roomed hut west of the main building. The hut itself is interesting, as it displays unusual brightly coloured symbols on the roof's overhanging front outside edge, said to be Maori symbols. The nearby enclosure was subsequently used to house captive badgers, including an ugly building of concrete blocks which had an underground chamber, which was utilised for studies of badger behaviour by Hans Kruuk and others. The main new building was added to the east part of the former house, but subsequently the house was totally destroyed by the great Brathens fire.

Any proposal to erect such a large new building in woodland well away from a settlement would be against local authority plans now and in recent years, as it would breach the policy of a presumption against new buildings in the countryside (other than for agriculture or forestry). However, this was before the oil boom, when development pressures were only beginning to rise in the Banchory area, and rents and house purchase were still reasonably cheap and easy to find. So, the proposal for a new building received planning approval. By the time that the Hill of Brathens building was ready in November 1972, the government had split the NC staff into a new Nature Conservancy Council (effectively the NC's former conservation wing), and ITE (the NC's former research wing plus some others).

DJ and the others to be transferred from Edinburgh moved up to the new station, and a big exodus to Brathens followed, involving most staff who had been based at Blackhall. In January 1975 Dr Hans Kruuk was appointed to take charge of research on vertebrate predators. He had been a DPhil student of Niko Tinbergen's at Oxford, along with Ian J. Patterson of Culterty, and both of them had simultaneously studied different aspects of black-headed gull/fox behaviour and predation at the then huge gull colony at Ravenglass in Cumbria. Hans had come for several days to see us at Aberdeen University, Blackhall, and both official and unofficial excursions up Deeside in spring 1969, after Robert Moss and I invited him to deliver a paper on his African predator-prey studies to the British Ecological Society's 10th Symposium.

The exodus from Blackhall to Brathens left at Blackhall the then grouse team of Robert, Ray Parr, David Watt and Bill Glennie who looked after the captive birds, and me. Also there as NC staff were Nick Picozzi studying raptors, typist Mrs Betty Allan, and Ray Hewson who now worked on foxes as a staff member of the Department of Agriculture and Fisheries for Scotland, supervised partly by DJ. There were also PhD students Hugh Kolb from England and Bryan Henderson from British Columbia (both working on grouse behaviour), and North American professors on sabbatical leave such as Dave Boag and Charley Krebs. Also at Blackhall were many visitors, including frequent ones such as Desmond Nethersole-Thompson, who was often with us in office, library and field while working on a NERC grant to write up his past ornithological work in the form of monograph books.

Based at Brathens, DJ began studying otters in the Dee catchment near Dinnet. Jim Conroy, who had done a post-graduate study at Culterty and later carried out biological research in Antarctica with the British Antarctic Survey, was appointed to take part in this work, and assistants were added later. Hans Kruuk was studying badgers near Loch Pityoulish in Strath Spey. This led subsequently to a PhD project there by Canadian student Paul Latour, and the American Jesse Boyce did PhD work on rabbits at Finzean, supervised by Hans.

Londoner Charlie Griffin, the first caretaker at Brathens, had previously lived with his wife at Netherton a short distance down the road towards Glassel. For some years he ran a small business with daffodils, obtaining bulbs too small for farmers to put on their markets and then selling them in small lots at the Banchory Show and elsewhere. The many daffodils that flower beside the roadway between Donnie's house and the station are a reminder of Charlie.

In 1974 the Rothschild Report heralded the advent of Thatcherite-like attitudes to science-funding before Thatcherism became a new word, and associated moves for 'rationalisation' (reduction in the number of an institute's stations and staff) increased in the late 1970s. Despite this, the grouse team at first managed to resist proposals to end the rental for Blackhall and move the team with Robert's captive grouse to Brathens. Eventually, the pressures from the top of NERC and ITE became irresistible, as small stations elsewhere were shut and their staff moved. We now had no Prof Wynne-Edwards to shield us, and the various good offers that I had had from North America had been taken up by others long before. Thatcherite attitudes to science had spread abroad as well as in the UK. Even a NERC Chairman, Hugh Fish, was a political appointee for favours rendered (former Chairman of Thames Water Board who had pleased Thatcher by aiding the formation of the first privatised UK water company). On his first visit to Brathens, he announced at the start of his pep talk that Great Britain Plc was now a leaner and fitter body because of recent political changes, and he saw NERC Plc of the future in like manner! Robert Moss and I had to give way.

Carrots intended to keep us happy were a new Brathens upstairs wing with two big rooms for Robert Moss and me, two smaller ones for Nick Picozzi and Raymond Parr, and a new hut and other new facilities for captive grouse in the nearby woods. The new upstairs wing totally escaped the subsequent fire. When I retired in May 1990 I vacated my room there to Hans Kruuk, but Bill Heal and Brian Staines asked me to remain at Brathens when I felt like it, on an emeritus basis. I moved to The Bothy, a wooden hut that had been erected as a small field laboratory at Mossside near Kerloch when the captive grouse were in an enclosure there. At Brathens it housed Ray Hewson as well as me, and later Jim Conroy and me, until the new post-fire building was ready. It now holds the freezers to the south of the long green hut. Nick Picozzi still has his original room in the upstairs wing.

Our last day at Blackhall was on Friday 20 November 1981. While writing this article I found the date, for I gave a lecture that evening on Aberdeenshire Gaelic at the Gaelic Society of Inverness, as is recorded in that venerable society's Transactions. After tea-time halfway through the morning, we put much redundant paper and files inside a rotten old henhouse, filling it most of the way to the roof, and then had a big bonfire. After lunch I drove to Inverness, returning on icy roads to Deeside in the wee sma oors of Saturday morning. As I did so, I recollected that a few of us knew of some interesting items that were probably consumed in the flames, including correspondence in 1963-66 that might well have resulted in the boot for a certain individual, but then maybe not, as "high heid yins" tend often to stick together, on the principle "there but for the grace of God go I"!

Robert Moss kept from the bonfire a wooden sign that announced "Blackhall Research Station", and later nailed it to the new grouse hut in the wood at Brathens. It is still there. He had arranged that when the hut was built it should have a little room where we could hold a small discussion group. Later the room was hardly ever used for the purpose, as the hut stood quite far from the main building, and was not well insulated and hence often cold. Shivering bodies and chattering teeth are not conducive to leisurely intellectual discussion! Although at first we thought it would be suitable on warm summer days, the room then became too hot, conducive to siesta rather than stimulating discussion. For all that, I remember an excellent discussion there on one occasion, when enthusiastic lively Norwegians from Bergen University Museum brought students to hear about the grouse work from Robert and me.

The rest you know about, or can easily find out, or can speculate about if you let your imagination run riot on what may have been in that rotten old hen-house!

Chapter 6. Lone ski-tours and climbs

When snow-patch enthusiast Iain Cameron and I first met at Crathes in December 2008, he mentioned my ski-mountaineering and asked "Have you published anything on them?" I said "I wrote a few articles for climbing-club journals decades ago". He asked for copies, and I sent three articles. Iain thought they should be read more widely. So, during 2009 in the website *winterhighland*, he posted the three. One was *Cairngorm langlauf*, a tour round the six main tops of the Cairngorms in April 1962. Later he posted *North Iceland on £10*, a trip to ski and climb in Iceland, and *Thirty miles on ski*, a tour from Gaick to Luibeg in April 1951. When he first suggested reproducing them, I judged that they would be of little interest nowadays. Iain thought differently, and, it proved, correctly. They did raise interest, and many modern skiers and climbers had been unaware of them. One of them, Jim Westland, suggested in a post on *winterhighland* that I should write a book about my early tours and climbs, and many others encouraged this with their own subsequent posts. My book *It's a fine day for the hill* (2011) was the result.

Among comments by them were surprise about my long tours alone, because in the 1940s to 1960s I lacked what they called today's benefits. The latter include light strong skis, sticks, skins, ice-axes, food, binoculars, torches, stoves, cameras, compasses, waterproof clothes, rucksacks, snow gaiters, boots, good ski waxes, accurate maps, reliable weather forecasts, courses, global positioning systems, mobile phones, flashing cameras, avalanche alerts, transceivers, and prior discussions about routes by email or internet with others who had already been there.

Helen Rennie I thank for writing about equipment and motivation. I had not thought it worth mentioning them, because to me they were so obvious, but she and Jim and Iain said I should. This chapter is a result. I include a few incidents from my book *It's a fine day for the hill*.

What I did on the hills was what I wanted to do, and I knew I would enjoy it. I did not do it to tell others, and did not write articles about it until others said that they would like to read them.

All of us should be learning every day. No one can know everything about ski-touring, climbing or snow, or know a hill as well as the ptarmigan or red grouse that lives on it. This is part of the wonder of exploring by your own free will. It is endless wonder

Snow and mountain-craft

At 86 years, I attribute what I know of snow and mountain-craft to seven lifetime factors.

1. From the age of five, determination.
2. From seven I noticed features and questioned their cause.
3. From seven an interest in snow expanded at 16-23 by climbing, glissading, Inuit dog-sledging, and ski-mountaineering, to knowing many kinds of snow and ice, effects on travel and avalanches, effects on plants and animals.
4. From eight I learned shapes of snow-patches, and began to record patches. By nine I knew shapes of hills and corries, and started rock climbing alone and unknown to anyone on small cliffs, by 12 was deeply interested in terrain, weather, using map and compass. By 19 this led to near-photographic memory of terrain and inherent navigation without compass or map.
5. At nine, Seton Gordon's *The Cairngorm Hills of Scotland* triggered a love of the Cairngorms and other mountains.
6. A research career that continued in retirement took me to the hill on weekdays and weekends, often in snow, sometimes at night, for over 60 years.
7. On the hill I was usually alone, attuned to snow, terrain and weather more than is possible in company.

Nevertheless I did appreciate good company. As a teenager I had many good days walking and climbing with my father and then with Tom Weir. Later I learned much about technical aspects of climbing on rock, snow and ice from Weir, Douglas Scott and Tom Patey. However, the grounding for my snow-sense and mountain-craft was set in my teens, on my own.

I did not find the hills a challenge, for I simply wanted to be there. The Cairngorms I came to know so well that when I saw them after absence abroad it was like seeing old friends again. Never did I find them frightening. I knew them too well and liked being there too much for that. In my teens I became confident in my ability to come off the hill in the worst of storms, even in white-outs so thick that I could not see my feet or skis, and had some difficulty breathing. Always I felt humility there, however, because the Cairngorms were so ancient and I knew I was but a fleeting visitor. After I was 19, I had the same feelings of love and friendship for bigger mountains, in Iceland, Sweden, Norway, Baffin Island.

Expensive elaborate equipment is not crucial for lone ski-tours and climbs

Above, I listed differences of equipment in the 1940s and 1950s compared with recent years. Equipment was heavier and less reliable, and weather forecasts poorer. Also above, I note other differences that made touring harder than now.

However, these differences are secondary, of little import. The primary requirements are to know where you are, to navigate by compass even when you cannot see your feet, to know terrain and weather, to enjoy feeling at home there. Also, determination is important, maybe over-riding. It induces confidence, which leads to further ability and so to more determination.

An example, heavy expensive Alpine skis and boots versus light cheaper Nordic skis and boots

Modern skis and boots for ski-mountaineering are heavy and expensive, but afford easier, faster downhill running than traditional narrow Nordic skis and light boots, and also provide greater safety if one falls. Obviously they are regarded as better than narrow skis for long steep descents in the Alps, whereas narrow skis come into their own for flat ground or gentle slopes. However, many Scottish mountaineers prefer the heavy equipment for higher Scottish hills such as the Cairngorms. There has long been inconclusive argument about which is better for the steep-sided high Scottish hills, Alpine versus Nordic. In the last decade, heavy equipment has increasingly tended to be favoured. However, in the last few years, the tour of the Scottish Haute Route by Roger Wild and his son Findlay, using light narrow Nordic skis and boots to cross the steep slopes from Ben Nevis to the Cairngorms, and then Roger's lone tour of the eight highest Cairngorms using the same light equipment, have re-kindled the flame for the Nordic equipment and its potential. Since the mid 1960s, it was possible to buy narrow wooden Norwegian skis in Scotland, and since the mid 1970s narrow plastic or fibreglass equipment from Finland, Sweden or Norway. The latter were tougher and less easily broken in a fall. However, I always found that wooden skis gave the best feel and the best guide to snow conditions.

Equipment and food

When I wrote this in February 2013, I had never owned a mobile phone or GPS or avalanche transceiver, or used any of them while skiing or hill-walking. In December 2013 I bought a mobile phone because our home phone land-line did not work properly for weeks, and occasionally not at all. Another reason was that it would be useful to keep in the car, in case of breakdown that I could not fix. I have never taken it on walks on the hill.

The serious danger of using mobile phones or GPS or avalanche transceivers when on the hill is that they inevitably detract from the above primary skills. Also they encourage some to go beyond their abilities and ignore portents of coming bad weather. It is too easy to phone local experts if tourists become lost, or even if they are not lost but wish information about the next pitch on a rock climb. A former member of of the Lochaber Mountain Rescue Team told me in the mid 1990s that a party on Tower Ridge in dry summer weather phoned several times to ask for information about the next moves that they should make on the route. On reaching the top they then asked how to find the path for descent to Fort William!

Vividly I remember walking with my three dogs up the snow-covered Feith Buidhe in June 1972 and finding the children's disaster bivouac, just beginning to be uncovered by a big thaw of the deep lying snow. I saw excellent sleeping bags, ground-sheets, spare clothing, stoves, fuel, much food, crampons, ice-axes, distress flares. What their group leader and officers in Edinburgh's education department lacked was common-sense and respect for the children of others, as well as sound experience of navigation and snow.

Even food is secondary, because a fit person who is used to being without it for most of a day on the hill can easily do without it for a whole day or longer without mishap. Of course food is important if you are going very long distances or ascents in a day on foot or ski. On the Gaick ski-tour, a big meal at Geldie Lodge and a rest for an hour out of the wind helped me decide to go further before night. Without that meal and good rest, I would have stayed at the Lodge and skied down the road to the Linn of Dee during the blizzard next day. That would have been easier, but less memorable.

Courses

Instead of attending courses, it is better to gain experience gradually on lower hills, next on high hills in summer, and only then venturing to lower hills in snow. Attendance on courses is likely to spoil or prevent the joy of exploring for yourself or with a companion. Also, it risks making you over-confident if you have little experience and understanding.

Some years ago, I recall that Braemar Mountain Rescue Team rescued a man on Carn an Tuirc near Glenshee ski centre. He became lost during a ski-tour on Carn an Tuirc, a hill near and in sight of the main road from Perth to Braemar. Newspapers reported that he had attended a ski-touring course at Glenmore Lodge a week before, and so that he was confident that Carn an Tuirc would be easy. The Rescue Team spokesman said that the man was an experienced cross-country skier, well equipped, and had taken the ski-touring course! To me his is a fatuous response that ducks what should have been said – criticism. Getting lost signifies incompetence. Even a beginner walker does not and cannot get lost if due attention is paid to terrain, weather, map and compass.

A recent example of getting lost appeared on 11 February 2013 in the *Press & Journal*. The newspaper reported that two walkers spent a couple of nights in snow holes at Coire Raibeirt of Cairn Gorm, after failing to return to their accommodation. The *Press & Journal* quoted the leader of Cairngorm Mountain Rescue Team, Willie Anderson, "They had dug themselves in after getting lost in mist and darkness. They were well equipped - they just got lost and did the sensible thing." Another fatuous comment that avoided the criticism which should have been made.

Next day the *Press & Journal* carried a report on an incident with seven members of Leeds University Union Hiking Club. One fell to his death in Coire an t-Sneachda while trying to help another who had

fallen but survived his fall and walked down to safety. The remaining five walked miles in the wrong direction to Carn Tarsuinn, a low hill above Dorback Lodge. 'Donnie Williamson, deputy leader of the Cairngorm rescue team, said the climbers had been well prepared, with crampons and helmets'. Yet another fatuous comment, economical with the truth. Yet the five were wholly unprepared on navigation, far more important than crampons and helmets. They alerted the police by mobile phone, saying that they did not know where they were, another manifestation of incompetence.

During early 2012, a man who had recently attended a course at Glenmore Lodge walked a few days later on a low hill by the Cairnwell, close to Glenshee Ski Centre. He claimed that he became disorientated when the wind blew the snow and mist came down. Yet he carried a compass and map. Disorientation is impossible if one has a map and compass and knows how to use them. Walking downhill would have quickly taken him to sheltered low ground and the road from Perth to Braemar. Instead, he dug a snow hole, having been instructed how to do so on the course, and spent some hours in it overnight. Then he used his mobile phone to seek rescue, was found by Braemar Mountain Rescue Team and walked with them to the car park. To the press he praised the course instructors, asserting that they had saved his life.

A better example of the adverse influences from courses would be hard to find. Instructors had taught him to dig a hole, but not the fundamentals of knowing terrain, weather, map and compass.

Route cards and similar information

For decades, politicians, police and mountain rescuers have warned that a person should never go alone on the hills, especially in winter. They decree that even parties of two or more must leave a route-card in a box at the foot of the hill or a note in a prominent place in their car, and tell others at hotel or boarding house or hostel or bothy what their planned route is and their time of return. I have never done this, and likewise Tom Weir who discussed it with me in 1947 and again in the 2000s. Many have landed in trouble, and a few even died, because they followed a planned route without foresight of the possible consequences.

Here is an instance that I well remember. For several deer-shooting seasons I worked during university vacations as a deer-stalking gillie at Derry Lodge. In September 1950, assisted by the Braemar police constable and an Inverey helper, I took my pony to carry the body of a man who had died of hypothermia at the summit of the Lairig Ghru. Why? After staying at Corrour Bothy, they had crossed the Dee in flood on a day of exceptional rain. The current swept one man out of sight downstream. Next day the police found him dead, washed on to a bank more than a mile downstream.

In shock after seeing him swept beyond help, his companions headed to the summit in torrential gale-driven sleet and wet snow. There they sat to rest a few minutes before the easier walk downhill towards Spey. One died where he sat, upright on a boulder. They had bought train tickets to go from Aviemore to Glasgow next day, which influenced them to stick to their planned route. Had they waited another day, as Mac Smith and other Aberdeen climbers in the bothy did, they could have crossed easily.

Safety

You are most likely to be safe if alone, and not distracted by conversing or being with others. Alone, you are far more vigilant and observant, aware of landscape, terrain, weather signs, wildlife and other interesting features. I go further and say that you are safest if you are aware that nobody knows where you are or where you are going. Imagine yourself alone on an Arctic icecap where no help will come if you make a mistake. Then you are inherently safer, and less likely to make that mistake.

Obviously no one can be 100% safe, because there is a possibility of a stroke or heart attack or lightning strike. However, even these (apart perhaps for lightning) are less likely when alone, if you feel good about being there. Even the risk of lightning may be less if you are alone than in a party offering a bigger target. If alone, you pay more attention to weather and are not competing with anyone. Hence you should be more likely to avoid going to places prone to a lightning strike, such as summits, ridges, tall trees and prominent sheltering rocks.

Chance or luck

Chance events such as changes in weather often affected whether I went on a long tour or not. For example, I intended to ski from Gaick to Deeside on 15 April 1951, not on the 14th. The fine morning of 14 April induced me to change my mind and go that day. If I had delayed my tour, the weather on 15 April was so bad that I would not have started the trip and would have returned to Turriff with my father. Likewise, if weather and snow had been less good on 23 April, I would have returned from Inverness to Turriff, instead of taking the train to Aviemore and skiing through Lairig Ghru to Luibeg. I did not plan any long tours meticulously beforehand, and started most on the spur of the moment, even on a whim. I think they were the more enjoyable because of that.

Determination

Determination, willpower, single-mindedness are related aspects of the same characteristic. They are crucial on long tours, especially if alone. As far back as I can remember, to the age of five, I have been determined about life and people in general.

When 10, I became seriously ill and nearly died. This was caused by empyema, before today's effective antibiotics and other drugs. Following surgery, I was in an Aberdeen hospital for nearly two months. On return home, I was off school for nine months, on the instructions of our general practitioner Dr James Hunter. Also he forbade gym, dancing, and football for two years. He told me I'd had a narrow squeak and would never walk the hills again, but could do gentle walking and look at the hills from afar. I did look at them in that first year from the higher parts of the Market Hill above Turriff and from the Brunt Smiddy on the Banff turnpike. I wanted more!

Determined was I to go to low hills soon, and then to the Cairngorms. In the end, will-power overcame physical weakness. Maybe the weakness aided the will-power.

Enjoyment of being alone

The above events at school reflected my being largely a loner. I liked being alone, and thinking and reading on my own. After I was 10 I attended the public library weekly and took books home as soon as allowed. I enjoyed being in the library and seeing the variety of books.

Near my grandma's cottage I climbed small crags when nine years old and drew sketches showing routes that I had climbed and others that I had not attempted because of their greater difficulty. I told no one till I left school years later, for fear that I would be forbidden. The crags were short, but jagged boulders lay below, and a fall would have caused serious injury and possible death. When 18 and with a longer reach and more experience, I returned to climb all the routes, and a few years ago likewise. The rock was a slate, unstable and steep. As a small boy I wondered why these crags were there. Only a few years ago I realised that they had been gouged by rivers during the melting of glacial ice.

Trips with my father and Tom Weir

My father started hill-walking as a result of my interest in it. By 1944 I had a better knowledge of terrain and navigating in mist than he. By the time that we bought our own skis and went ski-touring in early 1948 when I was 17, I had been for a week's hill-walking and ski-touring with Tom Weir at Luibeg. My father knew I had a better understanding of snow and ice than him, and when mist or snow white-out occurred he never said he should go in the lead to navigate and break the ski trail. He just accepted it when I confidently took the lead.

In February and March 1948 I was again on skis with Tom Weir. He had been crossing the Cairngorms alone on skis or foot, and going solo on other hills, and regarded this as normal and fine. I had thought this on lesser crossings, but his confidence increased mine. We shared a feeling that anything was possible if you are determined enough and are enjoying being there so much. We knew that we, alone or together, would always be able to get off the hill safely, under our own steam, no matter how bad the conditions.

Lone ski-tours on the Cairngorms

My parents had some worries about my lone trips, especially winter trips in my teens, but never showed this to me overtly. I am glad they gave me this freedom. It was a progression, because I first did a lone walk in the Cairngorms to Derry Cairngorm in summer 1943 when 13, and my first lone climb in winter snow to Morrone at Braemar in January 1947 when 16.

I first skied across the Cairngorms at New Year 1949 when 18, through the Lairig Ghru on a wild day of deep snow, hard frost and wind. By the time I left my parents in Aviemore on the previous late afternoon,

I hoped to stay the night in a shed at Coylumbridge and ski to Corrour Bothy or Luibeg. My father told me years later that he had slight but not serious concerns.

Many lone trips followed in 1949 and 1950 and 1951, as well as others when I accompanied Tom or my father or both, and occasionally I went with other Glasgow ski-mountaineers and Tom. By the time that I went on the Gaick trip, my father no longer had worries about me on my own. Indeed he envied my freedom.

Mountaineering and ski-mountaineering abroad

When 19 I made a trip abroad, in summer 1949 leading two other students to Iceland, and finishing with three days of lone climbing on glaciated mountains and one of ski-mountaineering alone on a glaciated peak. In summer 1950 I travelled alone to Finnmark in north Norway, Swedish Lapland, and Lofoten. I climbed in Lapland alone and in Lofoten with local mountaineers, followed by rock climbing and by snow and ice climbing on peaks in Lofoten and Lyngen Fjord with Tom Weir and Douglas Scott during July and August 1951. After they left I did lone climbing on the even steeper rock peaks of Moskenesøy in Lofoten during August 1951. In July 1952 I led two other students across Varanger peninsula in east Finnmark. Then in April 1953 I made a lone trip to the Avalon Barrens of Newfoundland for a week. Already in late 1952 I had been chosen to be zoologist on the Baird Expedition of the Arctic Institute of North America to Baffin Island in Arctic Canada during summer 1953, a progression of experience again.

In Baffin Island I was usually alone, amongst the finest mountains I had ever seen. Often I waded swift streams in the course of daily work, as well as travel on ice on lakes, rivers, fjords and sea. I crossed huge boulder-fields frequently, and occasionally visited uncharted valleys full of deep snow, on foot or snowshoe or ski. I travelled below enormous cliffs where rocks often fell, and glissaded happily on my own whenever the opportunity arose. Enjoying it immensely, I learned much from this and from travelling with the Inuit, who surpass us at coping with cold, damp and hunger. Despite having no map or compass, they never got lost. They just knew their world too well for that.

Lone climbs on rock resemble lone ski-tours in that if you make a big mistake you may die or be injured.

Lone trip ski-mountaineering from Luibeg to Rothiemurchus; Garbh Choire Mor in front, April 1951.

When doing my fieldwork on ptarmigan for a PhD degree at the University of Aberdeen in 1953 to 1956, and later, my main study area was Derry Cairngorm and often I went to Ben Macdui. For variety on the way up in summer and autumn I ascended rock routes on Coire Sputan Dearg. During fine dry weather, it was wonderful to climb leisurely up warm rough pink granite on Pinnacle Buttress, Flake Buttress or Crystal Ridge. The first two are moderate in standard, Crystal Ridge difficult, but I found the exposure on the moderate ones to be greater in some spots than on the more uniform incline of Crystal Ridge with its many small holds for feet and hands.

When alone, I never climbed these routes in winter conditions or routes of harder standard in summer. On some rocky ridges my father and I did not rope up, such as Aonach Eagach ridge or A' Chir ridge, and likewise when with Scottish Mountaineering Club members ascending or descending Curved Ridge on Buachaille Etive Mor. At such places and when walking above sea

cliffs, a moment's carelessness on easy ground can easily cause mishap or death.

Feeling frightened when alone
I did feel frightened as a boy, climbing alone on tall trees to birds' nests or on crags near my grandma's cottage. Most were very brief incidents. I recall once being frightened for several minutes in 1946 near Ballater beside a big stick nest at the top of a very tall spruce. To get above the nest and look in, I had to lean out with one arm hanging on the tree's main stem. Rain made the stem and branches wet and slippery. My legs shook on the upper branches below the nest, until I concentrated my mind on one careful move at a time, as one does on a rock climb or snow climb or a wade across a swift river.

I have felt frightened when alone in the Cairngorms and abroad, but only very briefly for a second or two each time, twice in the Cairngorms when cornices gave way near me in 1948 and 1949, once when climbing to an eagle's nest on unstable rock in 1948, a few times in Iceland when rotten rock gave way, and a few times on the steep grass of Lofoten mountains and Scottish sea-cliffs.

Once I felt fear longer than a few seconds, when making a solo crossing on a rope bridge without slings or karabiners, pulling myself against the friction from a wet rope, above a roaring deep swift glacial river in dense cold fog in Baffin Island at night in August 1953. I knew I would die if I fell off the rope. The answer was to concentrate, as with rock climbing, on the next move, a few inches forward each time and always getting closer to safety. Fear quickly declined and soon vanished.

Another risky incident in Baffin Island occurred when we assembled at an Inuit settlement to await an icebreaker to Montreal, this time not on my own. Half a dozen of us on a beautiful sunny afternoon set off by canoe to cross the fjord and inspect a cliff on the far side. On our return, the wind rose, waves swayed the canoe, and we came through a bout of white-water before reaching safety. Had the canoe overturned, we would have died quickly, strong swimmers or no, because of icy cold water. Again we concentrated on the next move, turning the bow into each big wave. I felt unsafe and unable to be in full control of my own actions because I was in a team and had little experience of canoeing. I felt concern, but not fear. Had the canoe overturned, I suppose I would have felt the greatest fear of my life, for a short while before oblivion from rapid hypothermia.

The nearest that I came to being killed was below Carn a' Mhaim in April 1948. I had been investigating slabs to see if they held an eagle nest. In my diary I wrote that I enjoyed a good standing glissade down a steep gully beside the slabs, on spring snow. After I left the crags and had already walked well down the slope towards the Luibeg Burn, I heard a loud noise behind me and turned immediately to look. A huge block of rock had become dislodged far above at the top of the crags. Crashing on to granite slabs, it broke into many fragments, which sped downhill like bombs. A large piece shot past very close to me, and then there came sudden silence. I did not have time to be frightened. Even had I had been wearing a metal hat, it would not have saved me if any of the big lumps had hit me, so it was just a matter of chance, hence luck.

On a day in late July 1949 in north Iceland, I skied

alone on a glacier under thunder clouds when I heard crackling and ticking nearby. My hair stood on end, and moved up and down. I judged that an electric charge was building, with a risk of lightning. When I moved away, the noises and feelings vanished. I had been apprehensive and curious, not frightened.

Fascination with snow

Snow has fascinated me since the age of seven. In later years, even when in snow so thick that I could not see my ski tips or boots, or had difficulty breathing, or could not stand and had to crawl, I found it interesting to observe snow and see what was happening. This happened when I was alone and in parties of two or three. The events became less worrying and threatening to me because of my interest in snow.

I recall discussing extreme conditions with Tom Weir and others. When crossing a pass from Monar to Achnashellach in winter snow, a severe gale blew Tom and Matt Forrester sideways along a slope of hard icy snow even though they were crawling on it. I had never experienced anything as bad, but Tom recounted it with interest as an unusual experience. He was a tough character, bodily and above all mentally. I learned much from him.

Early on, I found I could judge the reliability of snow or ice when walking or skiing on it, such that I did not fall through ice on ponds or snow-bridges across burns. I could tell the safety by listening to the water and judging the feel and sound of snow or ice under my boots or skis and in my bare fingers. If I judged it unsafe, I tried at a different spot nearby. Even on lowland at Turriff I walked daily in snow beside burns and ponds and the river Deveron. Skating on ponds helped gain experience, but the main understanding came from walking alone in snow and on icy backwaters and pools beside Deveron, especially in hard winters such as 1945 and 1947.

My father often fell through snow-bridges on foot or ski when alone, and so when he was with me he would let me go first because of my knowledge and confidence. Quickly I learned about the kinds of snow that provide not just the easiest and safest conditions for ascent and descent on foot and ski, but also the conditions that afford the most exhilarating and memorable skiing. It was as a lone skier that I learned and understood the scores of different kinds of snow

Lone trip to glaciers and peaks, Baffin Island, August 1953.

and ice that I came across. After some years I used to scan distant snow through binoculars, so as to judge what it would be like when I arrived there on skis. As a result, I would often divert from a straight line, so as to be on easier snow for ascent and descent, and thus expend less energy and above all incur greater enjoyment and appreciation.

Also, as I touch upon above, my snow sense has depended largely on being fortunate in having a research job which took me on to moorland and hill at all seasons and times of day, for many decades. Added to this was a deep interest for decades in how hill birds and mammals use different kinds of snow for shelter during the day and for sleeping in warmth and out of reach of predators.

Avalanches

It was a natural progression to learn the kinds of snow, weather and underlying ground that lead to avalanches and other kinds of slides such as slush avalanches and mudslides. I did not set off an avalanche on the hill, or became involved with one falling from above, but always liked watching avalanches and inspecting where they had already fallen, using binoculars to get closer views. The first one that I watched starting and finishing was a big one at Garbh Choire Mor in March 1948 when I was 17, on a sunny warm afternoon when a large cornice collapsed and thundered with a roar down the cliffs and gullies of the corrie, breaking into blocks up to 25 feet square. Since then I have watched scores taking place in the Scottish Highlands and have seen where many hundreds had recently taken place there, as well as in Iceland and Norway and Baffin Island. I did not kept detailed records on this, but have seen where avalanches had recently taken place in the Cairngorms during every month of the year except August.

Often during ski tours I used to check the snow when I had come down the main run at the end of the tour and had removed my skis to take a drink at a burn. At such places with a broad wreath affording a good run along one side of the burn, the snow next to the burn would be steep or even vertical or slightly over-hanging. Usually it would be anything from seven feet to 12 feet high. Often did I stand well back and touch the snow bank with the tip of my ski stick. I can recall the satisfaction of seeing and hearing the bank collapse with a loud hollow thump, at most covering my boots. That was a salutary lesson.

Since 1970 I have become more aware of the importance of ground-water and vegetation type in triggering the frequency and intensity of avalanches in Scotland. I should have been aware of it earlier, because in the late 1930s at Turriff I often saw deep snow sliding off slate roofs when a thaw had caused water to percolate down to the slates and thus under-mine the stability of the snow from underneath. Anyway, since 1970 I noticed that in many cases an avalanche began at a small spot where ground-water issued near a break of slope, the water having collected underground from gentler slopes above, slopes often forming large areas of plateau and summit. The avalanche at the starting point may involve a tiny area of instability, sometimes as little as a few feet across and deep, caused by lubrication of the under-side of the snow-pack by the ground-water. Once trig-gered, the instability can spread rapidly sideways and downhill. In many cases the ground-water may not be obvious at the surface except after heavy rain, but the vegetation type of grass rather than heath, again just below the break of slope, signifies the long-term effects of ground-water on plants.

Because grass affords far greater nutritive value to red deer than heath, red deer seek grassy vegetation caused by ground-water, and being below the break of slope affords the deer good shelter. As a result, hundreds of red deer have been killed by avalanches in Scotland. Some mountain hares have also been killed. Peter Fraser, former head gamekeeper at Glen Callater near Braemar, told me that in the late winter of 2010, a winter of many avalanches in Scotland, he saw where a big avalanche had swept down a steep slope on one side of the glen. It had been so powerful that it carried on across the wide area of flat ground in the bottom of the glen and had travelled uphill for some way on the far side. It had killed several mountain hares. This incident also is a warning that walking along the foot of a glen or even on the lower slopes above it on one side may not be safe if a big avalanche comes down on the other side of the glen.

I have never seen a red grouse or ptarmigan killed by an avalanche. With a daytime avalanche they would have plenty of time to avoid it by flying away. When roosting in snow-holes under the snow surface at night, one would expect them to be more vulnerable. However, they are acutely aware of noise and vibration through the snow, and quickly fly out if a person on foot or ski, a dog, or a piste machine comes close. As biologist Dave Mossop found in the Yukon, willow grouse under the snow at night are highly aware of the noise from an approaching fox, and all fly out to safety in the darkness, leaving the fox without a meal..

A smooth tract of short grass offers far less friction to snow than heath or other kinds of vegetation with many boulders. Hence an avalanche is more likely to start and more likely to be have greater effects. Even the kind of heath has an effect. Blaeberry loses its leaves in autumn, and so offers less friction to winter snow than the evergreen foliage of heather.

Another type of grassy vegetation that often occurs below a break of slope is the kind of snow-patch vegetation that is dominated by mat grass (*Nardus stricta*).On Scottish alpine ground it is usually short and smooth, again offering less friction than heath or vegetation with many boulders. This again leads to many avalanches. This includes some spectacular ones in spring. The weight of deep compact snow for months has flattened the grass, and with the first big thaw the melt-water percolates down through the spring snow to moisten the grass. The result is an avalanche right down to the surface of the grass. This seems to be a somewhat neglected field of study in the UK.

On the other hand, in Switzerland during 1982, Dr Fritz Schwarzenbach, then Deputy Director of the Swiss Federal Institute of Forestry in Zurich, told me of a decline in grazing by cattle and sheep on high alpine pastures in summer, owing to farmers abandoning traditional practices of taking stock to high pastures in summer and living there. As a result, grass on steep slopes had grown tall and rank. When winter snow came, it flattened the rank grass so that much grass lay like a smooth sheet with grass tips projecting downhill. Larger and more frequent avalanches had resulted.

Climbing alone on Trollafjall, north Iceland, July 1949, above Baegisarjokull (Baegisa glacier).

Interest in maps, terrain, vegetation and weather

From the age of nine onwards, coinciding with my interest in the Cairngorms, I became very interested in maps and developed an almost photographic memory of them. Likewise, on hills or coasts or woods or moors I quickly learned to remember terrain and vegetation, again almost photographic. Both abilities became useful if mist or storm came down, because they helped me to know where I was and how to return. However, I did not become interested in them or develop that interest because of reasons of safety. I did it because of interest in these subjects for their own sake. Later I recall discussing maps, terrain and vegetation with Tom Weir, Tom Patey and Stuart Rae, all of whom had a similar interest. We exchanged ideas and experiences, and learned from this.

A revealing point is how persons lay out maps when outdoors. Many turn the map round when facing south, east or west, often upside down as they face a particular view that they know well, such as from their house or the roadside. The above three and I always looked at a map the right way up, with north at the top and all the printing easily legible. Despite lifetimes living in the same place, most gamekeepers, shepherds and deerstalkers turn the map around if they are standing at their house or roadside and are looking south or east or west. A very few do not, such as John Robertson, ex-stalker at the Spittal of Glenmuick. He was exceptionally good at knowing and understanding terrain as well as maps.

Since the age of nine I have been interested in weather and clouds. Even if just shopping with my wife, I continually look at the sky and judge portents, such as a coming front. Almost always, others present have not noticed this. Fascinating to me are föhn conditions when a moist wind leads to sunshine in the lee of hills, sometimes as locally as a field, at other times affecting most of Deeside.

Navigation and orientation

In the early years I used a compass when in mist, and later found I could navigate accurately in snow and white-out by compass and map. However, with increasing knowledge of hills and navigation, I soon began to dispense with map and compass on hills that I knew well. On Ben Macdui plateau in summer, I learned to navigate accurately even with visibility down to 25 yards, without map or compass. By the time I was 21, I no longer carried map and compass even in winter storms on hills that I knew very well, such as my study area on Derry Cairngorm and nearby hills. Doing without map and compass increases your ability at navigating without them, because you continually learn new things about the hill, and realise that you did not know it quite as well as you had thought.

My interest in navigating increased in my teens and twenties and thirties. I saw for myself that plants orient themselves, and learned that I could easily know the direction in a large wood or forest by looking at lichens and moss on trees as well as plants on the ground, whether on a heavily overcast day or a starless night. I learned that ants arrange anthills to face certain directions likely to involve warm conditions. On subalpine and alpine land I realised that plants orient themselves

according to the direction of the prevailing wind, and again this is a remarkable and reliable feature.

By the time I was in my late 30s, and forever since, I was uncomfortable and felt unsettled on arrival in a strange new place, for instance after arrival on a starless night or a heavily overcast day, until I knew the direction of north. I would ask where it was. As soon as my host answered, or more so if I could look at stars or the sun myself, I relaxed immediately. In some where my host did not know where north was when I asked! I found it astonishing that anyone could live in a place for years and not know that.

My ability to navigate without maps in snow-less conditions on hills that I know well extended to places abroad that I had never seen before. I once flew to Amsterdam with a colleague who was not particularly interested in hill-walking or skiing, both of us heading for Arnhem to a scientific conference. There was no hurry and many trains plied between the two towns. However, when we entered the railway station. I quickly noticed that a train for Arnhem and later Germany was about to leave. Immediately I led the way unerringly along corridors and round bends, swiftly noting signs, and my colleague followed. We walked straight on to the train and it left within a minute. Had I not been with my colleague, he would have missed that train.

In 1970 I was at a conference in Helsinki, during which the field excursion involved a boat trip up the Gulf of Finland. We stopped at a Finnish town that I had never heard of, and the Finnish organisers told us we had an hour to be back on the boat before it moved to Helsinki. A US biologist colleague Gordon Gullion and I had been in animated scientific discussion on the boat, and this continued as we walked leisurely up the street into the town and stopped at street corners for further argument. After 40 minutes we suddenly realised we should be returning, but Gordon did not have a clue how to return, although used to being in the flat-tish boreal forest of Minnesota. I led the way, exactly retracing our steps along various streets and directions back to the boat, with ten minutes to spare. Yet I had not consciously noted street names or changes in direction on the way out. It must have just been something that my mind had absorbed without my paying any specific attention.

During July 1972 I spent a week in north Norway

In upper Glen Feshie, 14 April 1951, ski tour from Gaick Lodge to Luibeg,

with Svein Myrberget, who showed me his study area and research on willow grouse inhabiting the tiny isle of Tranøy. For a holiday two-day trip at the end, he, his wife and a local hill-walker and naturalist from the large nearby island of Senja went to Senja with me. In the afternoon of a glorious sunny day we hiked up a long wooded valley to a Lapp hut above a lake, near the tree line. We spent a night in the hut. Svein's intention next morning was to cross the mountains to a village on Senja's west side. The local man lived there, and would then take us in his car to where Svein had left his car on Senja's east side.

We climbed west, eventually into the alpine zone with mist and rain, among snowfields and boulder fields and small crags. I had never been on Senja and the local man was sure of the route. However, as time passed I became increasingly concerned that we were straying badly from a straight line or an approximation to one, and I said so. The local man dismissed this politely.

Eventually on descent after some hours, we began to come out of the mist, and a lake appeared dimly below us. I shouted with surprise and said "It's the lake we left this morning". The local man and Svein and his wife scoffed at this, saying there was a lake on the west side, but as we came lower, completely out of the mist, there was no doubt about it. Shortly we came to the Lapp hut! I think the local man took an anticlockwise movement in the mist instead of a straight line or fairly straight line. Anyway, we ended by returning down the valley that we had ascended the previous day, back to Svein's car.

Years later at the University of Trondheim I was external examiner for a PhD student. The University supervisors held a discussion with the student and me, and had asked Svein to come as a Norwegian pioneer in the student's subject. Before I spoke about the student's work, Svein introduced me by giving a personal recollection of my research and how he came to Deeside to visit me, and next how I visited him and his work. Then he recounted the trip across the mountains, and said it was the most remarkable ability he had ever witnessed in a person, that I continually said we were being led in the wrong direction and that I wanted to go in a different direction, without map or compass, simply from some inherent ability.

A region that I found difficult to judge was the flattish undulating tundra on the Avalon Barrens of Newfoundland in April 1953, just before I joined the Baffin expedition. I had a compass and a small-scale map of Newfoundland, both useful when the frequent fog rolled in suddenly from the Atlantic. However, in fine sunny weather I found it extremely hard to estimate the distances of ridges at anything from four-five miles away upwards. The map was no help, because it showed none of the ridges! Had I been there longer and had gone to the ridges, all would have snapped into clarity. It remained a conundrum to me. My purpose was satisfied by studying willow grouse, their habitats and vegetation within three miles or so of the hut. On one day I got a lift with a road-men's lorry to Portugal Cove on the coast, and walked back seven miles to the hut, but thick fog prevailed during the entire journey both ways, so I was no the wiser about the ridges. The conundrum made me vaguely discontent. I would have solved it to my satisfaction only if I had walked to the ridges and timed myself, but that would have taken a day away from my work and I could not afford the time for such a luxury!

Space-oriented behaviour appears to be more frequent in male than in female humans, and a likely evolutionary reason is that males were hunter/gatherers over wide countryside, whereas females tended to move less and be home-dwellers. Mountaineers and explorers tend to be male, and they will often admit that they enjoy male company on the hill and that female company can detract from the hunter/gatherer team spirit. Nowadays, such views are taboo to the politically correct, when we have legislation for gender equality and decisions to give jobs to women even where men are better qualified. It was interesting to me that my daughter young Jenny had a remarkably good ability at quickly understanding a strange new landscape, such as Vancouver when we went to live there in 1969 when she was 11 years old. She was better than her mother or our son of six years. Maybe there is sometimes an inherited component.

For decades I have been interested in the place names of Scotland, especially unpublished names that were at risk of dying out. I interviewed many hundreds of local indigenous folk to record their names. Most informants were men, as were all of the best informants. Again the wives tended to be home-dwellers, whereas the men worked in the wider countryside as deerstalkers, gamekeepers, gillies, farmers, foresters, postmen, salmon gillies, coastal nets-men, fishers off shore. Hence one could say that the men needed to know more place names than the women.

When I was at Turriff school on Deveronside, the primary and secondary schoolboys were again more adventurous, walking or cycling into the countryside to explore it, climb trees, find birds' nests, and catch trout, usually in small groups of two or three, though frequently alone. We did this off our own bat, for no one in authority such as parents, school teachers, church ministers, or leaders of the Boys Brigade promoted this. I cannot recall a single case of primary or secondary schoolgirls setting off in a group to explore the country, climb trees, or search for birds' nests. Perhaps this was a social taboo of the 1930s and 1940s, which has now been broken. I suspect, however, that there was and is an inherent evolutionary reason which helps explain and understand such differences in behaviour.

Eminent Swiss Arctic botanist Fritz Schwarzenbach worked in north-east Greenland during many expeditions. Fritz was an experienced mountaineer and ski-mountaineer, but the maps in north-east Greenland were small-scale and often inaccurate. When travelling alone into strange country, he writes (email February 2013), 'I tried to make a virtual film of the sequence of landmarks. Whenever I had reached a good landmark I stopped, observed the panorama of this point and checked the way I had gone. Memorising this "film" during the walk, I gained a good picture of the route I had chosen and come'.

Climbing alone in north Iceland, July 1949.

Innate behaviour involving orientation and terrain knowledge is a characteristic of man, as it unquestionably is of horses and dogs, let alone ptarmigan and hares that again do not get lost. Doubtless some individual humans are better endowed with it than others, as with any character. The attitudes that usually accompany modern civilisation can depress it or even eliminate it through learning of the wrong sort. The Inuit with whom I sledged did not need map or compass, and did not get lost. Nowadays, the Inuit for decades have lived in centrally heated houses, are well educated, and no longer use dogs except for taking tourists on paid trips. I wonder whether their superb ability to navigate without map or compass has declined, like those of most folk in modern countries further south.

Using a GPS to find where you are is one aspect of the depressing effect of modern civilisation on one's natural abilities at terrain knowledge and navigation, because if you are alert to terrain you should always know where you are, even in a white-out, from your compass line and your estimated speed of travel. However, there are too many so-called 'experts' on mountains and rescue, now including politicians. They tell people to use GPS, mobile phone and avalanche transceivers.

Using a mobile phone to seek help when you get lost and wish to be rescued is another depressing effect of modern civilisation on one's natural abilities. I have neither GPS nor mobile phone, though I do see a value for the latter if your car breaks down and you cannot fix it!

I have always been interested in my dogs' behaviour when I let them out of a vehicle. Take my current English pointer Henry. If I open the door of the car boot at a place he has never seen, at first he looks eagerly in different directions outside the boot door, and sniffs air deeply, taking big gulps of air. When I sign that he can jump out, he runs short distances at first, but secondarily soon quarters throughout a visible area within 300 yards, occasionally going out of sight in different directions but also turning to check my position. If I return to the same place on a later date, he displaces with the primary running. The earlier details are on a map inside his head! He has been on no course, and yet has a far better grasp of navigation than many people who attend courses and yet have not done the groundwork of getting to know terrain. Henry is better than me at understanding terrain in a strange place, if I am partly distracted by talking with others.

Of course dogs have an advantage over humans in possessing superb scenting ability. If they have gone out of sight of the human owner, they can quickly retrace their steps by following the scent on the outward track. They use this method even if it is not the shortest line back, until they see the owner or his vehicle. Then they make a beeline route back, delighted to be united again.

Wife and children

On my long lone ski-tours in April 1951 such as from Gaick to Luibeg or Luibeg to Whitewell, I was single. At the time of my intended attempt on the six main Cairngorms tops in February 1955 I was to be married three weeks later. During my intended attempt on the six main tops in April 1958 and actually skiing round four of them, my wife was pregnant and due to have a baby in July. At the time of my six tops langlauf tour in April 1962, I had a daughter almost four years old and another of a few months age.

None of this affected my decisions. If I had felt there was a serious risk of being badly injured or dying,

I would not have started on any of these trips in 1958–62. However, I was completely confident that I would be coming back not just in one piece, but better than before I started!

Taking equipment on tours

In the 1960s and 1970s I did more ski-mountaineering alone and in company, and likewise into the 1980s. I was then more experienced and more confident. Consequently, when on a long tour I did not take sleeping bag, groundsheet, survival bag, stove, pans, spare food and mug. I always carried ice-axe and crampons if I deemed them likely to be needed, but otherwise not.

If I judged that the weather was very settled with a big anticyclone, I did not take map, compass, anorak, over-trousers, or over-mitts. An example of this was a tour alone from the Cairnwell road at Glenshee ski centre to the Spittal of Glenmuick in 1975, via Glas Maol, Cairn of Claise, Tolmount, Fafernie and Broad Cairn, when my father dropped me at Glenshee and met me at the Spittal after skiing on Carn an Tuirc himself. When next day at Blackhall research station near Banchory a Canadian student Bryan Henderson asked where I had been and I told him about the settled weather and that I had not taken protective clothing, he raised an eyebrow and smiled, saying "Death wish?"

In fact, I was supremely confident of the weather and above all the terrain, and knew that I could come off the hill down to any one of a variety of glens quite easily. Indeed, on all the long tours, ending earlier and coming off the hill sooner was a possibility I could have followed, and would have followed had I become too tired or had the weather deteriorated badly or had I suffered a sprained ankle or worse by falling. On the Gaick trip, for instance, I could have returned to Gaick Lodge, or gone into Glen Feshie, or down Glen Bruar, or to the Tarf bothy and down Glen Tilt. In the article *Cairngorm langlauf* I mentioned how I considered coming off the hill earlier, on several occasions, such as down Glen Derry.

Interest in hills is akin to love

My feelings for snow and for the Cairngorms and other hills resembled falling in love, except that they continued long after the feelings that people commonly experience when first falling into sexual love. As early as my late teens, I occasionally felt a thrill sweeping over my body when I suddenly saw a beautiful place. It was not an orgasm, but perhaps had a similar neurological cause.

Here is an instance of it from my diary on 12 April 1950, after I had skied with a heavy pack from Glen More to Ben Macdui:- 'Storm was closing in all over Scotland, and there were grim views of black, grey and white clouds lowering on the hills. I left in a short furious blizzard and skied quickly to Loch Etchachan, a beautiful fast run, then down Coire Etchachan almost to the Derry crossing, wonderful snow all the way. It was queer to be in Glen Derry and see green grass in a burst of sunlight, and sit sunbathing a while by the Glas Allt Mor, it was all too good. I watched 200 hinds and calves grazing. Blue sky, sparkling snow and blue shadows, a big hailstorm and then a long clear spell as I reached Luibeg. The tops Beinn Bhrotain and the Monadh Mor shone with silver against the dark sky, the evening light was intense and sharp on the snowy hills, on the pines, and on the incredible blue of the burn. A pair of oystercatchers 'kleeped' joyously from the grassy flats and a cock crossbill sang close up near the lodge, burning red in the sun. What a kick one gets out of life at times, experiences so intense that a thrill of sheer joy runs all over one. Tired but happy, I arrived at Luibeg.'

On 15 May 1950 in Glen Luibeg, on the way up to ski on Ben Macdui:- 'Now the sun broke through and the first view of Ben Macdui from the path sent a thrill through me, the granite boulders glowing warm red in the sun, contrasting with snowy cliffs.'

Here is an instance when I sledged with Inuit hunter Samo and his dogs across sea ice. We were heading for Cape Searle Island. The sight of it elicited a thrill of feeling over my body, which I described in an article in the *Cairngorm Club Journal*:- 'Round the east end of Padloping Island we passed, below great red cliffs where the glaucous gulls shouted at us, and then out to the open sea. And then, around a corner, suddenly there rose a vast wall of towers and pinnacles out of the ice: Cape Searle. Samo announced "Kaxodluin!" the place of the fulmar petrels. A tingle of satisfaction ran over me. It must certainly be one of the most spectacular sea cliffs in the world.'

Perhaps this is a form of mental love, which engenders physical excitement and anticipation, and may help prepare for major physical and psychological effort. Certainly it adds to the experience.

At the end of our sledge trip, I had the prospect of crossing unexplored mountains. I can feel a touch of the tingles as I type this:-'Behind lay the sledge journey; ahead lay what? We could see a wall of great peaks rising from silky bowls of snow. I could feel awe, a touch of fear, and that vacant feeling in the lower regions that takes one before any big new undertaking, especially into country that is still a complete blank. Yet this as usual was a good tonic and I felt a tingle of exhilaration beyond measure. My only regret, and a great one, was the thought of leaving for good our great companion Samo and his faithful dogs. I wish I were back, riding the komatik again.'

If I knew that snow covered my home hills on a fine spring day, I have often wanted to be up there. If I could not go because of a meeting or other task already arranged beforehand, I felt slightly ill physically in my stomach, almost like sickness, especially if I looked at the distant hills, shining white in sunshine under a blue spring sky. Again I reason that the feeling is akin to love-sickness in a sexual sense, though in this case it had nothing to do with sexual feelings or a loved one of the opposite sex. But it powerfully affected me, and one result was that when I did get the chance to go to the hill a day or more afterwards, my desire and determination were enhanced. I have little doubt that this made the trip easier and more attainable, as well as more enjoyable. It has nothing to do with achievement in order to tell others. I get the feelings just as strongly when I tell nobody where I am going, and that applies to the overwhelming majority of trips on my own.

Physical fitness and psychological factors
Physical fitness is only one of the factors involved in a long solo ski-tour. Psychological factors are more important. To do long solo trips such as the Gaick one, it is necessary to be physically fit to a certain minimum, which I cannot muster at 86, and to have skills in skiing, navigation and mountaineering. However, though necessary, these are far from sufficient. Always required are determination, interest in snow and terrain, and a passionate sense of feeling at home in the hills.

Feeling at home in the hills
Ever since my boyhood reading I have been aware that a person who makes a serious mistake on a solo trip on

remote hills or glens in cold weather and winter snow is likely to die. If you feel at home in the hills, however, I believe that you are far less likely to make that mistake, and indeed you do not make it. Seeing familiar hills after long absence is seeing old friends again, and excitement and wonder come from just being there. I have always felt humility when on the hills. If you talk and think and write of conquering a hill or bagging a Munro or competing to be faster than others or expecting to tell colleagues of your conquests or hoping for media publicity or putting total reliance on GPS and avalanche transceivers and courses, I think you are more likely to make that mistake. All too many do make it.

I will never know all there is to know about even a few hills that I know best. Already in 1951 I realised that I will never match the ptarmigan's ability or the mountain hare's for knowing its home ground intimately, or for living and surviving superlatively there. The best I can do is share a little of their world, wonder about it, and admire it and them. I am a temporary poorly-endowed visitor to their domain. As a member of a species that evolved as a tropical mammal and still is tropical in physiology, I must soon terminate any visit to the heights, and return to renew my food, shelter and clothing in our unnatural though pleasant world of warm house, car, computer, shop, and above all the friendly human and canine and avian company at lower altitude!

At the end I give an addendum by returning to the Introduction to my book *It's a fine day for the hill*, published in February 2011, and I quote,'This book is testimony to the idea that *Exploring for yourself by your own free will, without formal courses or training, is the best joy the hills can give* (my Preface, *The Cairngorms*, 1975). Now I would add 'without detailed planning', for my best days have been lone trips begun without such planning, indeed on the spur of moment and weather, almost chance events.'

'Exploration by one's own free will is best pervaded by humility and wonder. Alien to this are avalanche alerts, 'challenge' walks, 'character-building', courses, Duke of Edinburgh Awards, guided walks, hill-runs, interpretive boards, marker cairns, outdoor centres, qualifications, rangers, route-cards, school outings, signposts, sponsored walks, tests of snowpack stability, text messages sent as avalanche alerts to mobile phones, transceivers, visitor centres, 'walk of the day', wardens, and 'wilderness walks'. Also alien are Munros, Corbetts and other anthropocentric designations, those who 'bag' them as if hills were shot birds, and assault, attack, battle, conquer, conquest, fight, vanquish and victory as if hills were enemies.'

Bibliography

Beament, J.W.L. (1979). Wildlife potential in Cairngorms. Landowning in Scotland 176, 124.

Duff, J. (2001). A bobby on Ben Macdhui. Leopard Magazine Publishing, Aberdeenshire.

Dulverton, Lord (1979). Wildlife potential in Cairngorms. Landowning in Scotland 174, 35–36.

Firsoff, V.A. (1949). The Cairngorms on foot and ski. Hale, London.

Gordon, S. (1925). The Cairngorm hills of Scotland. Cassell, London.

Grant, J.P. (1978). Wildlife potential in the Cairngorms region. Landowning in Scotland 172, 28–30.

Grant, J.P. (1979a). Wildlife potential in Cairngorms. Landowning in Scotland 174, 34–35.

Grant, J.P. (1979b). Wildlife potential in Cairngorms. Landowning in Scotland 176, 124.

Perry, R. (1950). In the high Grampians. Lindsay Drummond, London.

Poucher, W.A. (1947). A camera in the Cairngorms. Chapman & Hall, London.

Shepherd, N. (1977). The living mountain. Aberdeen University Press.

Watson, A. (1975). Dangerous thoughts on the mountain organisation-man. Etchachan Club Journal, issue named Penthowff, 1–19.

Watson, A. (1977a). Wildlife potential in the Cairngorms region. Scottish Birds 9, 245–262.

Watson, A. (1977b). Wildlife potential in the Cairngorms region. Scottish Birds 9, 390–391.

Watson, A. (1978b). Wildlife potential in Cairngorms region. Landowning in Scotland, 173, 36.

Watson, A. (1979). Wildlife potential in Cairngorms. Landowning in Scotland, 173, 36.

Wheater, R.J. (1977). Wildlife potential in the Cairngorms region. Scottish Birds 9, 389–390.

Essays on lone trips, mountain-craft and other hill topics

Some other books by the author

1963. Mountain hares. Sunday Times Publications, London (by AW & R. Hewson)

1970. Animal populations in relation to their food resources (Editor). Blackwell Scientific Publications, Oxford and Edinburgh

1974. The Cairngorms, their natural history and scenery. Collins, London, and 1981 Melven Press, Perth (by D. Nethersole-Thompson & AW)

1975. The Cairngorms. Scottish Mountaineering Club District Guide, published by Scottish Mountaineering Trust. Second edition published 1992

1976. Grouse management. The Game Conservancy, Fordingbridge, and the Institute of Terrestrial Ecology, Huntingdon (by AW & G.R. Miller)

1982. Animal population dynamics. Chapman and Hall, London and New York (by R. Moss, AW & J. Ollason)

1982. The future of the Cairngorms. The North East Mountain Trust, Aberdeen (by K. Curry-Lindahl, AW & D. Watson)

1984. The place names of upper Deeside. Aberdeen University Press, Aberdeen (by AW & E. Allan)

1998. The Cairngorms of Scotland. Eagle Crag, Aberdeen (by S. Rae & AW)

2008. Grouse, the grouse species of Britain and Ireland. Collins, London, New Naturalist Library No 107 (by AW & R. Moss)

2010. Cool Britannia, snowier times in 1580–1930 than since. Paragon Publishing, Rothersthorpe (by AW & I. Cameron)

2011. It's a fine day for the hill. Paragon Publishing, Rothersthorpe

2011. A zoologist on Baffin Island, 1953. Paragon Publishing, Rothersthorpe

2011. Vehicle hill tracks in northern Scotland. The North East Mountain Trust, Aberdeen, published imprint Paragon Publishing, Rothersthorpe

2011. A snow book, northern Scotland: based on the author's field observations in 1938–2011. Paragon Publishing, Rothersthorpe

2012. Some days from a hill diary: Scotland, Iceland, Norway, 1943–50. Paragon Publishing, Rothersthorpe

2012. Human impacts on the northern Cairngorms: A. Watson's scientific evidence for the 1981 Lurcher's Gully Public Inquiry into proposed Cairn Gorm ski developments, and associated papers on people and wildlife Paragon Publishing. Rothersthorpe

2012. Birds in north-east Scotland then and now: field observations mainly in the 1940s and comparison with recent records. Paragon Publishing. Rothersthorpe (by AW & Ian Francis)

2013. Place names in much of north-east Scotland. Hill, glen, lowland, coast, sea, folk. Paragon Publishing, Rothersthorpe

2013. Points, sets and man. Pointers and setters, stars of research on grouse, ptarmigan and other game. Paragon Publishing, Rothersthorpe

2013. Hill birds in north-east Highlands. Field observations over decades – ptarmigan, red grouse, golden plover, dotterel, bird counts. Paragon Publishing, Rothersthorpe

2013. Mammals in north-east Highlands – red deer, mountain hares, others. Paragon Publishing, Rothersthorpe

2014. More days from a hill diary: Scotland, Norway, Newfoundland, 1951–80. Paragon Publishing, Rothersthorpe

2014. Plants in north-east Highlands - timing of blaeberry growth, tree regeneration, land use, plant orientation. Paragon Publishing, Rothersthorpe

2015. The place names of Upper Deeside. Reprint facsimile of 1984 book. Paragon Publishing, Rothersthorpe

2015. Place name discoveries on Upper Deeside and the far Highlands. Paragon Publishing, Rothersthorpe (by AW and Ian Murray)

Lightning Source UK Ltd.
Milton Keynes UK
UKHW020722210319
339585UK00006B/50/P